The Smithsonian Guides to Natural America

THE NORTHERN PLAINS

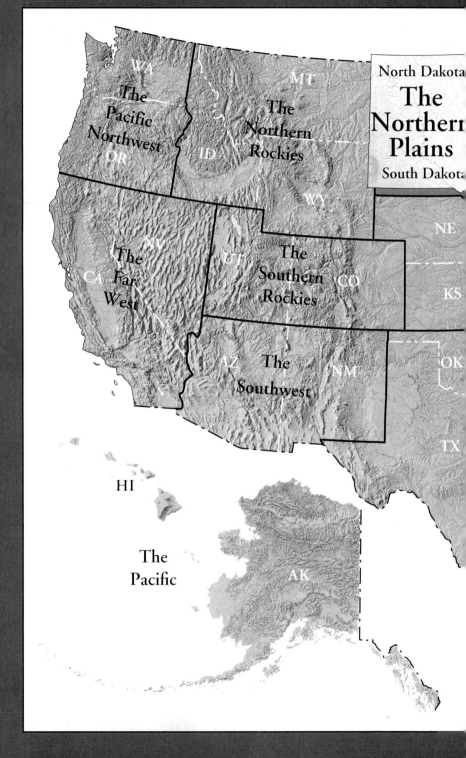

WA

The
Pacific
Northwest

OR

MT

The
Northern
Rockies

North Dakota

The
Northern
Plains

South Dakota

WY

NE

The
Far
West

NV

CA

UT

The
Southern
Rockies

CO

KS

AZ

The
Southwest

NM

OK

TX

HI

The
Pacific

AK

Minn

WI

MI

The
Great
Lakes

Northern
New
England

ME

VT

NH

The
Mid–Atlantic
States

NY

MA

CT RI

Southern
New
England

IA

The
Heartland

IL

IN

OH

PA

MD
DE

MO

WV

VA

The
Atlantic
Coast

KY

Central
Appalachia

NC

TN

The
South
Central
States

AR

SC

GA

AL

The
Southeast

MS

LA

FL

THE NORTHERN PLAINS
NORTH DAKOTA – SOUTH DAKOTA
MINNESOTA

THE SMITHSONIAN GUIDES TO NATURAL AMERICA

THE NORTHERN PLAINS

MINNESOTA, NORTH DAKOTA, AND SOUTH DAKOTA

TEXT
Lansing Shepard

PHOTOGRAPHY
Tom Bean

PREFACE
Thomas E. Lovejoy

SMITHSONIAN BOOKS • WASHINGTON, D.C.
RANDOM HOUSE • NEW YORK, N.Y.

Front cover: Tallgrass prairie preserve, Lake Benton, Minnesota
Half-title page: Bison, Theodore Roosevelt National Park, North Dakota
Frontispiece: Split Rock Lighthouse, Beaver Bay, Minnesota
Back cover: Wood duck; purple blazing star; American bison

THE SMITHSONIAN INSTITUTION
SECRETARY I. Michael Heyman
COUNSELOR TO THE SECRETARY FOR
BIODIVERSITY AND ENVIRONMENTAL AFFAIRS Thomas E. Lovejoy
DIRECTOR, SMITHSONIAN PRESS/SMITHSONIAN PRODUCTIONS Daniel H. Goodwin
EDITOR, SMITHSONIAN BOOKS Alexis Doster III

THE SMITHSONIAN GUIDES TO NATURAL AMERICA
SERIES EDITOR Sandra Wilmot
MANAGING EDITOR Ellen Scordato
SERIES PHOTO EDITOR Mary Jenkins
ART DIRECTOR Mervyn Clay
ASSISTANT PHOTO EDITOR Ferris Cook
ASSISTANT PHOTO EDITOR Rebecca Williams
ASSISTANT EDITOR Seth Ginsberg
COPY EDITORS Helen Dunn, Karen Hammonds
FACT CHECKER Jean Cotterell
PRODUCTION DIRECTOR Katherine Rosenbloom

Library of Congress Cataloging-in-Publication Data
Shepard, Lansing.
    The Smithsonian guides to natural America. The Northern Plains—
  Minnesota, North Dakota, South Dakota/ text by Lansing Shepard;
  photography by Tom Bean; preface by Thomas E. Lovejoy
       p.   cm.
    Includes bibliographical references (p.260) and index.
    ISBN 0-679-76477-1 (pbk.)
    1. Natural history—Minnesota—Guidebooks. 2. Natural history
  —North Dakota—Guidebooks. 3. Natural history—South Dakota
  —Guidebooks. 4. Minnesota—Guidebooks. 5. North Dakota
  —Guidebooks. 6. South Dakota—Guidebooks. II. Bean, Tom.
  II. Title.
  QH105.M55S48 1996   95-9040
  508.978—dc20   CIP
Manufactured in the United States of America
98765432

How to Use This Book

The Smithsonian Guides to Natural America explore and celebrate the preserved and protected natural areas of this country that are open for the public to use and enjoy. From world-famous national parks to tiny local preserves, the places featured in these guides offer a splendid panoply of this nation's natural wonders.

Divided by state and region, this book offers suggested itineraries for travelers, briefly describing the high points of each preserve, refuge, park, or wilderness area along the way. Each site was chosen for a specific reason: Some are noted for their botanical, zoological, or geological significance, others simply for their exceptional scenic beauty.

Information pertaining to the area as a whole can be found in the introductory sections to the book and to each chapter. In addition, specialized maps at the beginning of each book and chapter highlight an area's geography and geological features as well as pinpoint the specific locales that the author describes.

For quick reference, places of interest are set in **boldface** type; those set in **boldface** followed by the symbol ❖ are listed in the Site Guide at the back of the book. (This feature begins on page 267, just before the index.) Here, noteworthy sites are listed alphabetically by state, and each entry provides practical information that visitors need: telephone numbers, mailing addresses, and specific services available.

Addresses and telephone numbers of national, state, and local agencies and organizations are also listed. Also in appendices are a glossary of pertinent scientific terms and designations used to describe natural areas; the author's recommendations for further reading (both nonfiction and fiction); and a list of sources that can aid travelers planning a guided visit.

The words and images of these guides are meant to help both the active naturalist and the armchair traveler to appreciate more fully the environmental diversity and natural splendor of this country. To ensure a successful visit, always contact a site in advance to obtain detailed maps, updated information on hours and fees, and current weather conditions. Many areas maintain a fragile ecological balance. Remember that their continued vitality depends in part on responsible visitors who tread the land lightly.

CONTENTS

PREFACE

The Northern Plains region of natural America encompasses far more than the term *plains* usually brings to mind. Here in Minnesota and the Dakotas lies the midcontinental transition from forest to plains as well as the upper reaches of such major drainages as the Mississippi, the Missouri, and the system that gives rise to the Saint Lawrence. For me this region has always been evoked by the paintings of Francis Lee Jaques, many of which are in the collection of the Bell Museum of the University of Minnesota.

If you know the area's geology well, you can see the handiwork of glaciers almost everywhere. In eastern Minnesota, for example, the 40-mile moraine where the twin cities of Minneapolis and Saint Paul now stand, along with the large sandplain to their north, mark the place where the last ice advance stalled some 14,000 years ago. In western Minnesota, vast Glacial Lake Agassiz (named for the famous Swiss-born Harvard geologist who served as one of the Smithsonian's first regents) was bounded on one side by the glacier and fed by its meltwaters. The waters ultimately broke through their boulder-choked southern drainage in a torrent known as Glacial River Warren, cutting a channel for what is today the Minnesota River. Elsewhere old strandlines still mark the shorelines of Lake Agassiz.

As is often seen in previously glaciated areas, the eastern part of the Northern Plains is strewn with lakes and ponds—as if Jackson Pollock had bespattered the landscape working only with azure hues. So be prepared to paddle a canoe if you want to truly experience this part of natural America. On my "must" list for the region is a trip to the Boundary Waters Canoe Area Wilderness to see and hear the wildlife of the North, including wolves and loons. From this abundance of aquatic habitats comes one of this country's great natural delicacies—wild rice, long savored by Native Americans and introduced to the rest of the world principally by the forebears of Roger Kennedy, current director of the National Park Service and previously distinguished director of the National Museum of American History.

This region boasts the largest of all North American bodies of water, Lake Superior. Occupying a natural trough of Precambrian rock, Superior is so large (400 by 160 miles) and so deep (up to 1,333 feet) that it creates its own local weather systems. A barrier to migration for large birds such as hawks (which need thermal air currents, generated only over land), the

PRECEDING PAGES: *As the moon rises, the setting sun delicately tints the forest-topped western wall of Slim Buttes in northwestern South Dakota.*

lake forces them to follow a migration corridor around its western end. The wetlands of the region are similarly important to a midcontinental migration used by 75 percent of all canvasback ducks, as well as by many other waterfowl. With more than half the original wetlands now gone, any further loss is a matter of concern for the future of migratory waterfowl. On Superior's north shore Grand Portage National Monument commemorates the 3,000-mile fur trading route known as the Voyageur Highway, which itself follows a trail established even earlier by Native Americans.

In northern Minnesota stands what is left of a once-vast conifer forest. Today, although greatly altered, these woodlands can still be seen and appreciated for what they were. The forest of jack pine, spruce, and balsam fir also includes white and red pine, as well as some northern hardwoods, aspen, and birch. A good place to see this northern woodland is Itasca State Park, named for the lake at the headwaters of the mighty Mississippi, which, of course, is integral to Longfellow's *Song of Hiawatha.*

Farther south is a transition to a hardwood forest composed mostly of oaks, and farther west a transition through the oak savanna region to real prairie beyond. Dominated by fire-resistant bur oak, the forest-prairie boundary has been very dynamic, shifting with the changes in climate as well as with the effects of fire, once deliberately set by native Plains tribes.

People tend to think of the prairie as boredom all the way to the horizon. Nothing could be further from the truth. The prairie is alive with myriad forms: tallgrass with big bluestem, Indian grass and cordgrass; medium grass with needlegrass and needle and thread; short-grass with blue grama, prairie Junegrass, and buffalo grass. And that is not all: black soil prairie, dry sand prairie, gravel prairie, hill prairie, bluff prairie, and more—each supports its own distinctive flora and fauna. One fine example of this ecosystem is Minnesota's Ordway Prairie, commemorating a member of one of the century's most ardent conservationist families. In Minnesota's southwestern corner is the Prairie Coteau highland, draining on its western side into the Missouri and on the eastern to the Mississippi. In its lower parts the Coteau forms a wet prairie, populated with bluejoint and northern reed grass, rare Dakota and Ottoe skipper butterflies, and a full palette of wildflowers.

In North Dakota the flatlands are relieved by wetland-sprinkled highlands, the Missouri Coteau, the Prairie Coteau, and the Turtle Mountains. The first comprises the heart of what has been called the duck factory of the nation because of the bounty of its watery potholes and despite its paucity of rivers. More than ducks benefit, however; this highland also shelters piping plover, Baird's sparrow (named for the second secretary of the Smithsonian) and even white pelicans. In the northeast corner of the state the Pembina Gorge region includes the longest and deepest unaltered river

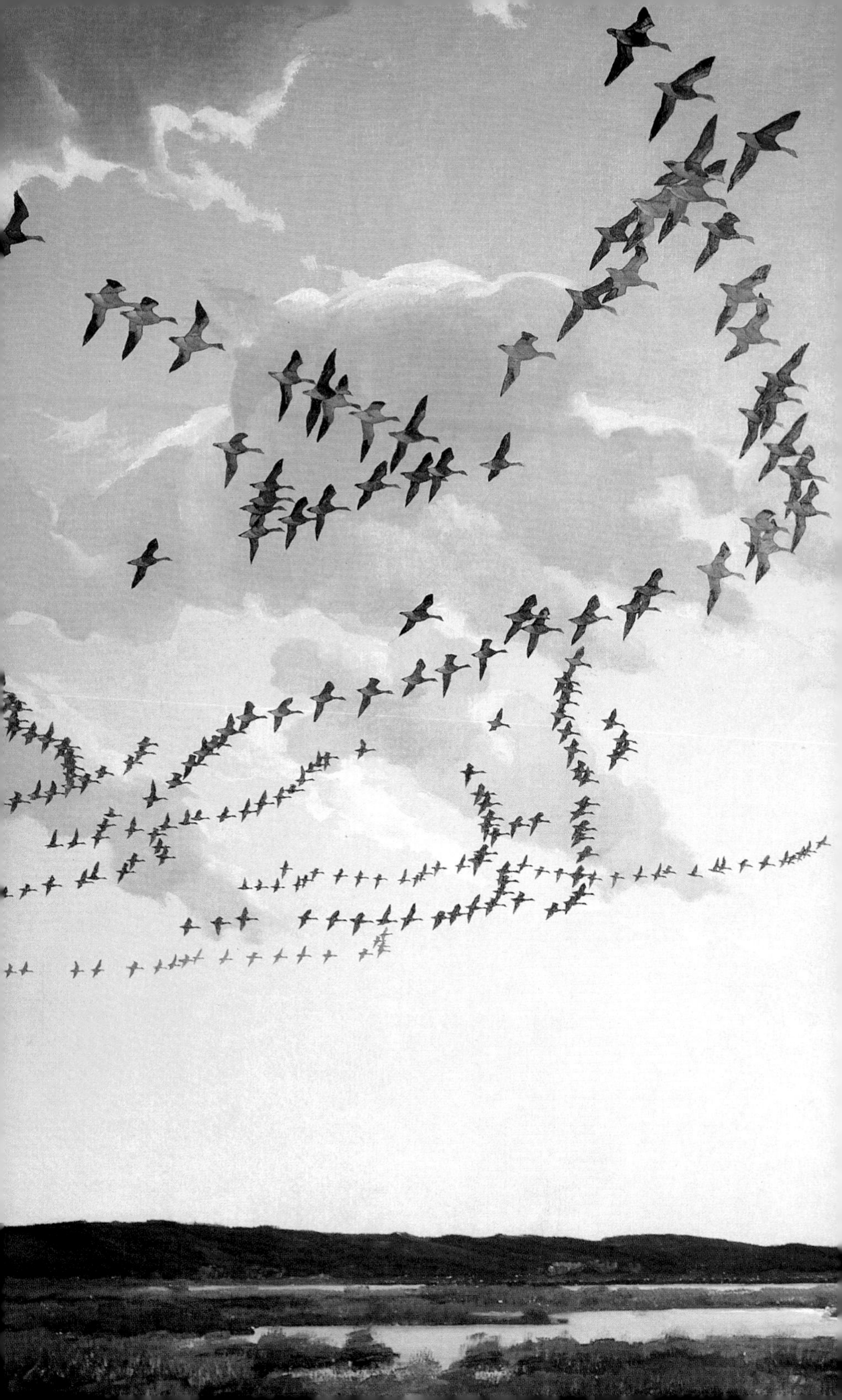

valley in North Dakota—another great place for that canoe. And if you look carefully, you might find one of the world's smallest flowering plants, the southern watermeal. Farther west, national wildlife refuges—Des Lacs, Upper Souris, J. Clark Salyer, and Lostwood—showcase a diversity of birds from marbled godwits to snow geese.

Southwestern North Dakota is the butte and badland country that attracted 25-year-old Theodore Roosevelt in 1883. Today two-sectioned Theodore Roosevelt National Park commemorates his love for the area's "vast silent space." In the park's South Unit, Painted Canyon is a riot of geological color. Some of the color comes from lightning-ignited seams of lignite that bake the clays, shales, and sandstones. The badlands are bighorn sheep country, but only a tiny number hang on.

Agriculture now dominates 90 percent of South Dakota, but the state still harbors interesting elements of natural America, ranging from part of the Prairie Coteau to the badlands. Sand Lake National Wildlife Refuge is a major staging area for snow geese. Westward is fine fossil country, source of many of the great dinosaur finds.

South Dakota's greatest treasure is the Black Hills, a 6,000-square-mile forested haven rising above the surrounding plains. Its Floral Valley so impressed General George Armstrong Custer that he wrote extensively of it in his diary; given the violence surrounding him it seems odd yet comforting that for a brief moment the cavalry rode with bouquets in hand. Of the 72 calcite-crystal caves in the world, 68 are found in the Black Hills, and Wind Cave is the world's seventh largest limestone cavern. Finally there is Mount Rushmore, the image of which is engraved in every American's mind.

Today much of the Northern Plains has been transformed. The native Audubon bighorn sheep was hunted to extinction. Gone too are the great herds of bison, the grizzlies, elk, caribou, and passenger pigeons.

Still, go to Minnesota and see why Francis Lee Jaques entitled a painting that depicts an ax embedded in a stump with a chickadee pertly perched on its handle *The Optimist*. Like photographer Tom Bean, you will find much to admire on the Northern Plains. And you couldn't have a better guide to this part of natural America than my good friend Lansing Shepard who knows and loves it well.

—Thomas E. Lovejoy

Counselor to the Secretary for
Biodiversity and Environmental Affairs,
SMITHSONIAN INSTITUTION

LEFT: *Great wavy lines of migrating snow geese dominate a prairie wetland in Francis Lee Jaques's* **Wings Across the Sky,** *painted about 1935.*

THE NORTHERN PLAINS

50   0   50 Miles
50   0   50 Kilometers

International
Falls

Upper Red
Lake

71

Mesabi Range

53

61

LAKE SUPERIOR

Fargo

10

71

MINNESOTA

35

Duluth

94

Mille
Lacs
Lake

WISCONSIN

St Cloud

12

St Paul

71

Minneapolis

14

MISSISSIPPI

29

90

90

RIVER

Sioux
Falls

35

I O W A

71

29

INTRODUCTION

INTRODUCTION

THE NORTHERN PLAINS

If one could pick a place on the North American continent where *the* East becomes *the* West, the northern Great Plains would be an excellent choice. To travel the 550 miles from the Saint Croix River valley on the border of eastern Minnesota to the westernmost reaches of the Dakotas is to move from a well-watered landscape of green farm fields and lush deciduous woodlands reminiscent of New England or Pennsylvania to the dry, deeply cut canyon-and-arroyo rangeland of a Hollywood western. This dramatic transition results from the region's central position on the continent and from the landscaping of mile-thick moving ice.

Lying approximately midway between the North Pole and the equator, the states of Minnesota, North Dakota, and South Dakota are swept by fronts of polar air from the Arctic and bathed by warmer systems drifting north from the tropical Gulf of Mexico. Average temperatures in the region's northern and southern reaches are vastly different. Weather here is often distinguished by seasonal extremes: very hot summers and frigid winters.

Here, too, geography has a profound effect on what gets watered, and hence on what grows where. Drained of moisture on their ride over the Rockies, prevailing westerly winds have little rain left to shed on the region's arid western sections. As the clouds continue to move east, however, they gather water again from the warmer Gulf air wafting north up the Mississippi basin. Thus the region is generally dry in the west and wetter in the east, warm in the south but significantly cooler in the north.

At the Missouri River, the soils of the northern Great Plains go through an equally dramatic transformation. To the west, the land lies over worn shales, clays, and sands—the nutrient-poor floors of vanished seas, rivers, and swamps. Weathered and eroded over millions of years, this is classic western terrain: dry rolling plains dissected by countless draws. Silted rivers course through eroded badlands, which fan out along their length. Punctuating these high, parched prairies, isolated buttes rise on the flats and uplands, providing little nourishment for water- and nutrient-hungry plants.

East of the Missouri, on the other hand, lie some of the richest soils on the

---

PRECEDING PAGES: *At sunset, a small island seems suspended between water and sky in Lake Kabetogama in Minnesota's Voyageurs National Park.*

RIGHT: *A western meadowlark pours forth a lilting melody. Physically identical to the western species, eastern meadowlarks are distinguished by their more whistlelike song.*

planet. Here a thick mantle of mineralized rock deposited during the last ice age is covered by several feet of rich loam, the decomposed biomass of an immense, unbroken prairie that had been accumulating for nearly 10,000 years. The process began some 25,000 years ago when the last in a succession of continental glaciers came grinding out of Canada, burying nearly all the region east of the Missouri. Advancing and retreating as the climate alternately cooled and warmed, the ice worked and reworked the land. It flattened old highlands, excavated river valleys, deposited new highlands, flooded lowlands, and cut trenches for rivers where no rivers had flowed before. When it finally melted about 9,000 years ago, the ice left an immensely varied landscape. Across the western two thirds of the region lay a huge glaciated plain: Undulating land interrupted by isolated ranges of high hills where the ice had stagnated, and great stretches of flat lake plain, where giant pools of meltwater had formed ponds. In the east lay a chaotic jumble of hills—lateral and end moraines—the debris left by successive advances and retreats of the glacial fronts. Nearly all of it was shot through with water—tens of thousands of lakes, pools, ponds, potholes, and wet depressions. The landscape was primed for the rich mix of biological life that would later occupy it.

During the 100 centuries that followed, vast forests (remnants of which still thrive today) rose in the region's wetter eastern sections. In the cool far northeastern corner of Minnesota, a shifting mosaic of conifers came to blanket the rocky terrain, intermingled with great swaths of northern hardwoods and aspen-birch. Primeval in appearance, these woods were the southern extension of an immense forest that once extended unbroken across the top of the continent between the Bering and Labrador seas.

To the south, firs, pine, and spruce give way to sugar maples, American basswood, and a wide variety of oaks—red, white, and black oak, northern pin, and bur. Cloaking the hills of southern Minnesota, these trees represent the western edge of a vast eastern deciduous forest that spanned most of the continent east of the Mississippi in presettlement times.

Along these forests' western edge, a narrow buffer zone of brushland and oak savanna formed a transition landscape that lay between the forests of the

3

east and the enormous interior grassland to the west. Extending from the Canadian border to Texas, it was an ecosystem always on the move. Shifting eastward over the millennia during warm, dry periods and westward during cool, wet ones, this singular landscape was largely maintained by the prairie fires that regularly swept in from the west. Ignited either by lightning or by Plains tribes, who drove game before the flames, fire would roar east, burning back all woody vegetation and clearing the underbrush. Of all the species in the eastern forest, only bur oak, with its tough, fire-resistant bark, could withstand these constant conflagrations, and thus this tree came to dominate the savannas. (Today farmlands cover much of this region, but where prairie is being restored, fire again maintains the ecological balance.)

West of the oak savanna lay the northern prairies, a sea of billowing grasses that decreased in height as they swept westward to the Rocky Mountains. At the eastern edge stood tallgrass prairie, dominated by six-foot-high big bluestem, Indian grass, and prairie cordgrass. Farther west, the vegetation adapted to drier conditions. Across the James River valley and the great drift plain of eastern North Dakota, three-to-four-foot mid-grasses such as needlegrass and needle-and-thread joined and finally eclipsed the tallgrass. By the eastern slope of the Missouri Coteau—the rumpled morainic highland that runs east along the length of the Missouri River—short grasses such as blue grama and prairie Junegrass grew. Beyond the Missouri, where rain becomes less frequent, short-grass species dominated until on the dry, poorly drained plains and broken badlands of the westernmost counties, the prairie mix shifted to the hardiest short-stemmed types such as buffalo grass and blue grama.

Today, these grasslands are greatly altered, replaced in the east by cash crops, and inundated in the west by a sea of exotics—many of them imported forage grasses: European brome, cheatgrass, Kentucky bluegrass, and a host of others. Nevertheless, enough of these original prairies still survive, especially in the west, to keep intact a semblance of this grand succession.

All told, from east to west, the forests and grasslands present a neat ecological sequence—except for one large anomaly in the southwest corner of South Dakota. The Black Hills constitute a landscape unlike anything around them. An uplifted and eroded dome of granitic and sedimentary

RIGHT: *Along the Caribou Trail above Lake Superior's North Shore, sugar maples in fall attire signal the arrival of another Minnesota winter.*
OVERLEAF: *A spring storm gathers over South Dakota's Badlands National Park; in summer this savanna is bone-dry, its grasses golden.*

rock, the Hills are a dark green forested island in an ocean of grass. Compared to the surrounding plains, the climate is cooler in the summer, warmer in the winter, and wetter year round. The soils of the elevated Hills, derived from igneous and metamorphic rock, sustain an ecosystem dominated by ponderosa pine on the higher slopes; bur oak, elm, and green ash on the lower slopes; and prairie vegetation in the foothills. A unique mix of plants and animals coexist here, including species from the surrounding grasslands, from the western ponderosa pine forests, from the northern spruce-fir woods, and from bur oak–dominated forests to the east.

Across the region, all these ecosystems once supported an unbelievable abundance of wildlife. The wooded east was home to caribou, lynx, marten, wolves, fishers, moose, elk, deer, black bears, beavers, and mountain lions. Across the plains wandered vast herds of bison counted in the millions and innumerable elk and pronghorn. Wolves roamed the entire territory, and grizzlies, mountain lions, and bighorn sheep ranged through the badlands of both Dakotas and along the Missouri. And abundant birdlife was everywhere: eagles, cranes, and upland game birds. Immense flocks of passenger pigeons periodically descended on the forests of the southeast, and across the prairie, migrating flocks of ducks, geese, and shorebirds gathered in numbers that sometimes obscured the sun.

Before the arrival of European explorers, these woodlands, prairies, and highlands were home to many different groups of native peoples, descendants of the Paleo-Indians who had crossed the Bering Strait from Asia in prehistoric times: Cheyenne, Ponca, Pawnee, Assiniboin, Fox, and Crow, among others. Earthen lodges of the Arikara, Mandan, and Hidatsa stood along the Missouri, bark lodge villages of the Ojibwa dotted the upper Mississippi, and throughout the woodlands and across the prairie as far as Montana and Wyoming, rose the conical bison-hide tepees of the Sioux.

Today both human and natural landscapes have changed dramatically. The Native American settlements—along with a centuries-old lifestyle—are long gone. The members of these tribes—whose forebears survived the smallpox and cholera epidemics of the 1700s and 1800s and the Army-Indian wars of the late 1800s—are now concentrated on reservations. The bison are gone as well, along with the enormous herds of elk and pronghorn. The grizzlies have vanished, as have the native bighorn, the tallgrass and most of the mid-grass prairies, the red and white pineries of the northeast, the caribou, and the passenger pigeons. Immense flocks of plover, curlews, canvasbacks, scaup, and many other waterfowl, shorebirds, and upland prairie birds no

ABOVE: *In 1832 Karl Bodmer, a Swiss artist with the Maximilian expedition, painted this watercolor of the upper Missouri near Fort Union.*

longer roost in such numbers in the pothole-ridden uplands. Most of the big maple-basswood forest of the southeast has disappeared, as have more than half of the prairie wetlands and nearly all the wolves. The Missouri River lies under a chain of impoundments created by massive earthen dams, and even the Mississippi is more a lake than a river along much of its upper reaches.

There *are* places, however, where bits and pieces of the world observed by Meriwether Lewis and William Clark at the beginning of the nineteenth century can still be found today, poignant reminders of the price modern society pays for the way its people live. In parks, monuments, and sanctuaries, on grasslands and in forests, endangered animals and plants thrive in protected environments, and threatened habitats have a fighting chance. The region abounds in history and beauty: from the craggy, wooded shoreline of Grand Portage on Lake Superior to the vast, delicately tinted reaches of Badlands National Park, from the solitary buttes of the northern plains to the pastel-colored bluffs overlooking the Mississippi River. For travelers with a sense of adventure and an eye for landscape, Minnesota, North Dakota, and South Dakota present a wild and spectacular natural wonderland, just waiting to be discovered, explored, and savored.

MINNESOTA

PART ONE

M I N N E S O T A

Minnesota is a land of grand conjunctions and major ecological transitions. Here three of North America's principal
biomes converge, producing a region rich in ecosystems
and habitats. Positioned near the center of North America, the state enjoys
a diverse climate—high temperatures in the south and frigid readings in
the north—and moderate precipitation, which diminishes in the west. The
enormously varied topography is a forceful reminder of the awesome prehistoric power of continental glaciers on the move.

Three major American river systems originate within Minnesota. The
Arctic-bound Red River of the North composes the state's western border
with the Dakotas. The Mississippi rises in the north-central highlands and
flows along the state's southeastern boundary with Wisconsin before bisecting the continent in its rush toward the Gulf of Mexico. In the northeast, myriad streams emptying into Lake Superior collectively form the
headwaters of the Atlantic-bound Saint Lawrence River.

In the drier, western reaches of the state lies a treeless expanse of cultivated fields—what was once tallgrass prairie and the eastern end of a great
grassland that stretched to the Rocky Mountains. By contrast, dense woodlands flourish in eastern Minnesota. In the cooler, wetter northeast, northern
coniferous forest—northern hardwoods mixed with evergreens, birches, and
aspens—predominates; in the southeast, sugar maples, American basswood,
and red oaks are the mainstays of an eastern deciduous forest.

Spattered across the face of Minnesota are thousands and thousands
of lakes. Starting near Lake Superior in the northeast, they form cascading
chains that sweep across the land in arcing bands, trailing west and south
across the state. These lakes are the tracks of successive glaciers that began
invading the region some 100,000 years ago. The piled debris they left be-

---

PRECEDING PAGES: *Once the domain of the Sioux, the rolling green terrain
above the Mississippi in southeastern Minnesota is now dotted with
tidy farms. Here cattle graze peacefully under an early morning mist.*

hind has given form and character to the hilly, wooded landscape throughout this part of Minnesota.

The vast, barely undulating plain of southwestern Minnesota presents a marked contrast. Here ice sheets deposited a thick mantle of mineralized soil some 300 feet deep. For centuries tallgrass prairie with few trees and even fewer lakes thrived on this terrain, which today supports corn, soybeans, wheat, and barley. Running southeast like a saber cut across this portion of the state is the wide, deep valley of the Minnesota River, sliced by the force and volume of an ice-age deluge called Glacial River Warren. Rising at Browns Valley, just east of the South Dakota border, the Minnesota drains a vast lowland stretching away to the southeast.

The torrents of water that roared down River Warren originated in one of the world's greatest glacial lakes. Named for Louis Agassiz, the nineteenth-century Swiss naturalist and father of modern glacial theory, Glacial Lake Agassiz once covered most of northwest Minnesota. Blanketed in tallgrass and wet prairie across its southern and western reaches, and with aspen, brush prairie, and wetlands farther north, the big lake's pancake-flat lake plain has today been converted to farmland. In its northeastern sections, however, the glacial lake bottom has remained much as it was centuries ago: a vast region of wetlands and impenetrable peat bog—a wild, roadless wilderness of spruce and tamarack forests, cedars and sphagnum moss.

A world away to the east lies the rock-bound border lakes country and the wind-swept north shore of Lake Superior. Backed by a range of high forested hills, the dark basaltic rim of the Superior basin rises above the icy waters of one of the world's largest and deepest freshwater lakes. From surrounding highlands—some as high as 2,000 feet above sea level—numerous rivers cascade over boulder-choked chutes into the lake below.

Some 900 million years after the volcanic Superior basin had hardened, the younger blufflands of southeastern Minnesota—now home to the majority of the state's population—were formed. This deeply dissected high plateau is composed of layers of sediments laid down by successive inland seas. Although the ice from the last glaciation spared this region, rivers swollen with glacial debris carved wide steep-walled valleys across this plateau, the grandest of which is the majestic bluff-lined valley of the Mississippi River, which dominates the southeastern fringe of the state.

Today much of Minnesota's landscape has been clear-cut, plowed, dammed, drained, and asphalted for human use. Still, nature does persist in special places that have important and fascinating stories to tell.

CHAPTER ONE

MINNESOTA'S SOUTHERN TIER:
BLUFFLANDS, BIG WOODS, TALLGRASS PRAIRIE

From the metropolitan area surrounding Minneapolis–Saint Paul to the Iowa border, southeastern Minnesota is dominated by the Mississippi River. Constituting part of the state's eastern border with Wisconsin, the Mississippi winds its way through wooded islands, backwater channels, sloughs, and marshes. More than four miles across in some places and bracketed by towering 600-foot sandstone and dolomite bluffs that glow tawny in the evening light, this stretch of great river takes one's breath away. Where the bluffs end, steep-sided hills dominated by oaks, maples, and basswood tumble down to the river plain. Rushing streams drain the hills, flowing through woodlots, pastures, and a landscape of small farms not unlike Vermont; trout streams ripple through deep, wooded valleys and narrow limestone coulees.

Ascending the hills to the west, the closed forest of the river valley yields to open plain and an intermediate landscape of wooded draws and fields. About 150 years ago, this strip of highland was a mixture of brushland, woodland, prairie, and patches of bur oak, part of a transitional zone separating the eastern forests from the western prairies that extended from southern Canada to the Gulf of Mexico. In Minnesota, this landscape was maintained by fires ignited by lightning or set by Native Americans who used the flames to drive bison, elk, and other game.

LEFT: *Forming the border between Wisconsin and Minnesota, the Mississippi flows through the Black River delta near La Crosse. Here countless islands, marshes, and channels lace the Upper Mississippi refuge.*

This whole area—roughly from the Mississippi River west to I-35, and from south of the Twin Cities to the Iowa border—is the northwest corner of a Paleozoic plateau, a 10,000-square-mile highland that spreads over neighboring sections of Illinois, Iowa, and Wisconsin. Composed of the stratified fossil floors of numerous seas that came and went between 600 million and 350 million years ago—well before the age of dinosaurs—the highland has been deeply eroded by streams and chemical weathering. Although it spared this area, glacial ice still had a profound effect on the land. As the northern ice sheets melted, enormous volumes of debris-choked water surged east toward the Mississippi, cutting the deep valleys of the region's major streams—the Root, Zumbro, Whitewater, and Cannon—and carrying glacial drift, which formed the deep, rich soils that produced prairies, savannas, and croplands.

Bounded on the north by the Minnesota River and on the east by the morainic hills along I-35, southwestern Minnesota is an open and nearly treeless land. This gently rolling glacial plain was the northeastern edge of North America's vast interior grassland, which stretched west to the Rockies. Less than 200 years ago, it supported a rich variety of habitats: wet prairie and sedge meadows in the swales, black-dirt prairie on the uplands, and in special places, dry-sand prairies, gravel prairies, and hill prairies. Today, almost all of it has been converted to corn, soybeans, wheat, and barley.

The land here was carried from Canada and North Dakota on the back of the last ice sheet and deposited in thicknesses up to 400 feet atop the fossilized mud and sand floors of inland seas that predated the glacier by some 900 million years. Two landforms break the monotony of this region. One, a flat-topped plateau, rises nearly a thousand feet above the surrounding plain in the extreme southwestern corner of the state. Called the Prairie Coteau, its eastern edge is defined by a range of rolling hills extending from the town of Burr on the South Dakota line southeast to the town of Jackson. The Coteau is a bedrock highland covered by a thin layer of glacial debris older than

OVERLEAF: *Evening sunlight burnishes the native grasses of the Nature Conservancy's Hole-in-the-Mountain Prairie in southwest Minnesota. It takes nearly 600 years for such a tallgrass prairie to reach maturity.*

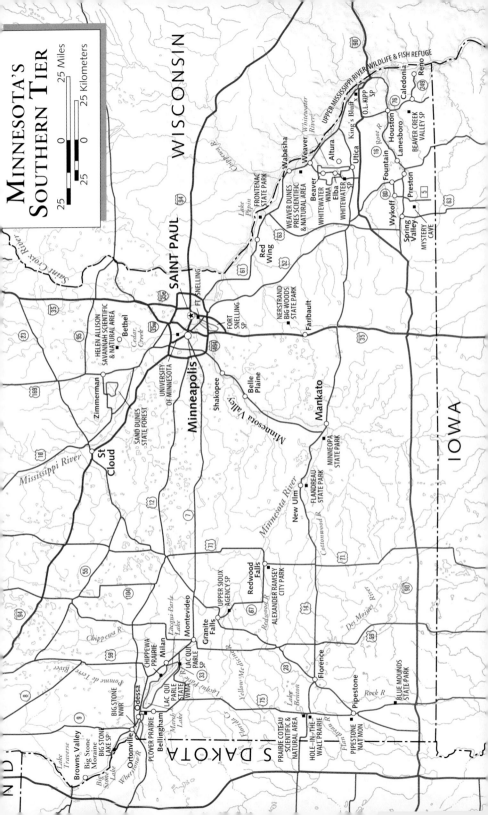

ABOVE: *American artist George Catlin (1796–1872) painted* Pipestone Quarry on the Coteau des Prairies *in 1836–37. The Plains Indians have long carved ceremonial pipes from the soft reddish siltstone mined here.*

the surrounding plain. The steep, rolling hills that line the Coteau's base and stand high along its eastern crest are the piled debris dumped by the last ice sheet that was forced to go down the side of the plateau. Bedrock here is a Precambrian sandstone called Sioux quartzite, a pinkish metamorphosed rock that appears prominently between the towns of Luverne and Pipestone. The famous pipestone quarries run along an exposed vein of the reddish pink siltstone that has been used by Native Americans for more than three centuries for their ceremonial pipes.

The other significant landform on these southwestern prairies is the broad valley of the Minnesota River. Rising near the town of Browns Valley on the South Dakota border, the river runs some 332 miles southeast to its confluence with the Mississippi at Fort Snelling. The Minnesota's channel was carved by the released contents of Glacial Lake Agassiz, a massive body of water that became impounded between a land divide and the melting ice sheet to the north. When the rising waters finally topped the divide, the deluge, called Glacial River Warren, cut a nearly straight trench—where the Minnesota flows today—up to 5 miles wide and 250 feet deep through glacial till, sedimentary material, and in some places, all the way down to the continent's Precambrian foundation rock.

Beginning in the state's southeast corner, this chapter follows Route 61 north along the west bank of the Mississippi River through Hastings to the Twin Cities and the confluence of the Minnesota and Mississippi rivers at Fort Snelling. Then it heads down Route 169 to Mankato and generally northwest up the Minnesota River valley to Browns Valley. The journey ends in the southwest corner of the state with a short tour of Pipestone National Monument and special sites on the Prairie Coteau.

BLUFF COUNTRY

A touch of the fabulous enlivens the drive north on Route 61 from the Iowa state line along the western side of the Mississippi River. High bluffs and dramatic forested hills plunge to the edge of the highway, which winds along the river. Across the Mississippi's floodplain, wooded islands, sandbars, marshes, and the glinting waters of myriad backwater channels stretch over the vast valley floor. In the distance rises the eastern wall of the valley and Wisconsin.

This riverine landscape is part of the **Upper Mississippi River National Wildlife and Fish Refuge❖**, some 200,000 acres of floodplain extending 260 miles southward along both sides of the river from Wabasha, Minnesota, nearly to Rock Island, Illinois. Occupying one of North America's great avian migration corridors for species moving north and south, the refuge is also an important sanctuary for many plants and animals that have been nearly eliminated from the surrounding human-dominated terrain.

Among the marvelous variety of wildlife living in or passing through the refuge are some 290 bird species, 40 percent of North America's waterfowl and shorebirds, 57 mammal species, 45 species of amphibians and reptiles, 118 species of fish, and 37 species of freshwater mussels, probably the continent's most endangered group of animals. Although the bison, wolves, elk, bears, and pronghorn (often mistakenly called antelope) are gone, beavers, muskrat, mink, weasels, foxes, white-tailed deer, and some 40 smaller nongame mammal species still roam the river bottomlands. Northern pike and bass ply the backwaters, and large bottom feeders such as carp, buffalo fish, and sheepshead support a commercial fishery. Represented here as well are

ancient lineages harking back to the age of dinosaurs—notably gar, lake sturgeon, and bizarre spatula-beaked paddlefish.

The amazing diversity of birds traveling this corridor during spring and fall migrations makes this area special to birders. More than 30 species of warblers, as well as bald and golden eagles, hawks, ospreys, and turkey vultures typically pass through this ribbon of water and woods, and 25 species of ducks, geese, grebes, and herons are found here during migration. In the fall, some 75 percent of the continent's entire population of canvasback ducks fly this corridor, and thousands of migrating Canada geese and tundra swans gather in huge flocks along favored bays and side channels.

Although barge traffic on the Mississippi's main channel can make the open waters perilous for small craft, good canoeing and shallow-draught boating (access points dot both sides of the river) are possible along the backwater channels and in the marshes and sloughs that edge long stretches of the river. Maps covering 30-mile sections of the Mississippi from the Iowa border to the headwaters at Lake Itasca are available from the Minnesota Department of Natural Resources in Saint Paul or from refuge headquarters.

Despite its wealth of wildlife, this ecosystem hangs in the balance.

Among the waterfowl migrating along the Mississippi Flyway are graceful northern pintail (far left); canvasbacks (top left), speedy flyers with quick wing strokes; and wood ducks (bottom left), which nest in trees in the river bottomlands.

Continuing shoreline development, industrial and municipal waste discharge, and 29 locks and dams threaten the health of the river. The locks and dams have created a string of impoundments, called pools, that have inundated the floodplain's wetland, forest, and slough habitats. When shallow sediment-filled lakes are stirred by the wind, the suspended sediments appear to reduce the light penetration that aquatic vegetation needs to grow. Declines in aquatic vegetation in turn degrade insect, waterfowl, and fish habitat. Federal plans to consider deepening and widening the channel of the upper Mississippi to facilitate increased barge traffic have led natural-resource managers of five states to warn that this vast ecosystem may be on the verge of collapse.

One of the best roads into the high country from Route 61, Route 249 west from Reno to Caledonia offers a scenic ride up the narrow, winding valley of Crooked Creek. Five miles west of Caledonia on County Route 1 is **Beaver Creek Valley State Park❖,** set in one of the region's myriad preglacial drainages that was enlarged and deepened by meltwater pouring off the glacial front to the west. The valley's bedrock sides, composed of a layer of sandstone packed between two layers of dolomitic limestone, rise 250 feet above the creek floor.

The woods here are classic mesic hardwoods, sugar maple, basswood, walnut, and oak on the uplands, and floodplain species such as willow, box elder, elm, and cottonwood on the valley floor. In dry, rocky places along the valley's crest, small stands of juniper and pine cling to a precarious existence. Numerous springs seep from the porous

LEFT: *Partial to a shady spot in sandy soil, the showy lady's slipper—the tallest of North America's native northern orchids—flourishes in the woodlands of Minnesota.* **RIGHT:** *Although heavily logged by European settlers, the woodlands of the Root River valley have rebounded. Here sunlight brightens a trail in Forestville State Park.*

rock layers, and wildlife is abundant. Besides ubiquitous raccoon and white-tailed deer, badgers, muskrat, beavers, mink, and occasional wild turkeys roam the woods. Timber rattlesnakes—one of the state's two poisonous species—are found here as well but are not common. A known warbler hot spot among birders, the park offers an opportunity to observe Acadian flycatchers, cerulean warblers, and Louisiana waterthrushes, species more common in other parts of the state. Beaver Creek supports substantial numbers of brown trout and enjoys a reputation as one of the state's better trout streams.

Route 76 north to Houston is a gorgeous winding drive into the heart of the bluff country that traverses narrow, wooded river valleys and rolling farmland. From Houston, Route 16 west to Preston follows one of the region's prettiest river valleys—the home of the **Root River,** a major waterway draining the plateau and one of the most popular canoeing spots in southeast Minnesota. A state hiking and biking trail winds above and along the stream between the town of Fountain in the west and Money Creek woods, just east of Rushford. Outfitters in Lanesboro offer canoe, tube, bike, and ski rentals. The upper Root meanders beneath high sandstone and dolomite cliffs topped by oak and shagbark hickory. At this birding mecca, more than 200 avian species that regularly appear include bald eagles, ospreys, turkeys, a variety of hawks, turkey vultures, great blue herons, and common egrets. The Root is home to several state-threatened fish species at the northern edge of their range: the bluntnose darter, black redhorse, pugnose minnow, gravel chub, and nonpredaceous American brook lamprey.

Just west of the town of Preston is **Forestville State Park,** offering

trout fishing and hiking trails among wooded valleys.

A strange pitted landscape punctuates the agricultural uplands of this region. A short drive west on Route 80 from Fountain to the town of Wykoff offers what appear to be islands of stunted trees set amid rolling open fields. Closer inspection reveals that only the trees' upper halves are visible, rising from holes about 30 feet deep and 30 to 150 feet across. In this karst country—where irregular limestone contains caverns and underground streams—the funnel-shaped depressions are sinkholes; upward of 5,700 populate this region, and more open each year.

The plateau here is underlain by porous limestone, which dissolves in the presence of weak carbonic acid. As rain falls, it collects atmospheric carbon dioxide and becomes slightly acidic. When this rainwater seeps into the ground, its acidity increases as it gathers more carbon dioxide from the soil, air, and rotting plant tissue. This weakly acidic water dissolves the limestone. Following fractures and the interstices of the porous rock, the seeping water then literally eats away the plateau's interior. Deprived of its bedrock underpinning, the ground above collapses into sinkholes. Karst topography has reached its highest degree of development here. Perhaps the most dramatic consequence of this process is **Mystery Cave❖**, six miles southeast of the town of Spring Valley off County Route 5. A testament to the

ABOVE: *Nervous and timid, the omnivorous red fox is generally nocturnal. With a heavy coat well suited to winter, the fox often beds down directly in the snow.*

LEFT: *The golden light of early morning bathes the hilly limestone terrain of southeast Minnesota's cave-and-sinkhole region.*

creative powers of chemical weathering, this wet limestone cave contains more than 13 miles of known passageways, and more are being discovered. Among Minnesota's nearly 300 identified caves, Mystery is the largest and most diverse. Its formation probably began in the Cretaceous period, some 100 million years ago, when its rocks were deposited, and the cave itself is probably 500,000 to 1,000,000 years old. Today

ABOVE: *Once shot as poultry predators, red-tailed hawks are now protected, abundant, and often spotted above the state's southeast blufflands.*

it features stalactites, stalagmites, brightly colored flowstones, and many fossils: brachiopods, cephalopods, trilobites, and graptolites. The south branch of the Root River passes through its lower level, and during dry years the whole tributary literally disappears into the cave.

Visitors who wish to envision the grand scale of the glacial forces that shaped the continent—particularly this corner of Minnesota—find **O. L. Kipp State Park❖,** just north of the I-90/Route 61 interchange, particularly illuminating. (From Route 61, take County Route 12 north and County Route 3 to the park entrance.) High on the bluff tops above the wide Mississippi floodplain, the 3,000-acre park is a land of sheer-faced, half-domed scarps, steep, thickly wooded valleys, and rolling green uplands. More than six miles of hiking trails traverse the site, many affording splendid overlooks; a fine self-guided nature trail leads to King's Bluff, a major promontory providing a spectacular vista. The unobstructed view across the valley from here, some 500 feet above the

RIGHT: *Surrounded by hardwood forest, a small goat prairie occupies a bluff top above the Mississippi floodplain at O. L. Kipp State Park.*
OVERLEAF: *The Whitewater River winds beneath limestone cliffs in Whitewater State Park; the river's South Branch is a fine trout stream.*

LEFT: *A summer resident, the handsome prothonotary warbler haunts the region's moist bottomland forests, often nesting in old woodpecker holes.*

RIGHT: *Autumn leaves and bright green duckweed, a floating plant that is fodder for fish and waterfowl, carpet a floodplain forest in Frontenac State Park.*

river, allows visitors to imagine the immensity of the roaring deluge that sliced its way through this vast plateau some 12,000 years ago. Enormous volumes of water and rock debris from the melting ice farther north and west cut a 700-to-800-foot trench—some 100 to 200 feet below the present floodplain. In the millennia since, the sediment-laden river, greatly slowed and vastly diminished in size, has steadily continued to refill its bed.

On these bluffs, thick stands of maple and basswood cover the steep north-facing slopes, and red, white, black, and northern pin oak trees—many quite old—dominate the drier east-facing inclines. Shagbark hickory also grows here, at the very northern limit of its range. Botanists are drawn to the park because of the unusual plants that perch precariously on several dry, steep south- and southwest-facing slopes. Called goat prairies because only goats can reputedly negotiate the 40-to-50-degree incline, these grassy patches of prairie grasses and forbs support rare communities of wild indigo and jeweled shooting star. Squirrel corn, at the northwest edge of its range, can be found in the protected parts of the park. Opossums, red foxes, and the increasingly rare spotted skunks are among the 35 mammal species found here. Birds include a number of large charismatic species: wild turkeys, ruffed grouse, great horned owls, both bald and rare golden eagles, turkey vultures, and red-tailed hawks among others.

Perhaps the best place to experience the full range of southeast Minnesota's diverse ecosystems is the 28,000-acre **Whitewater Wildlife Management Area**❖ and adjacent 1,750-acre **Whitewater**

ABOVE: *In Minnesota's southeastern woodlands, a scalloped turkey-tail fungus (top) helps decompose a dead log; the uncommon timber rattlesnake (bottom) is one of the state's two poisonous snakes.*

State Park❖, which lie along Route 74 in the valley of the Whitewater River. Native Americans named the river for the water's milky color during spring floods, when light-colored clay eroded from its banks. Stretching from the town of Weaver along Route 61 in the north to about two miles north of Utica in the south, the two units include both the river's lower reaches and its upland tributaries.

In the south, the Whitewater's feeder streams—the South, Middle, and North forks—twist and turn under high cliffs, converging at the town of Elba. On the uplands above the valley, especially to the west, oak forest gives way to bur oak and grassy clearings. Steep bluff prairies grow on the south- and southwest-facing slopes, maintained by controlled burns. Algific talus slopes—small unique habitats of accumulated rock debris with permanent ice in the rock crevices—lie

ABOVE: *Cottonwoods grow at Frontenac State Park. Such blufflands harbor some 30 natural plant communities and support more than 100 rare species, making the region the state's most botanically diverse.*

under the magnificent cliffs that rise majestically above a stretch of the Middle and North Forks. Deep limestone coulees and steep-sided goat prairies occur there as well. Whitewater WMA supports a rare dry oak savanna, which provides habitat for a number of state-endangered species: sea-beach needlegrass, Ottoe skipper (a butterfly), rough-seeded fameflower, and goat's rue.

Along the Whitewater, floodplain forests grow on the bottomlands. Two fine goat prairies can be explored on the south-facing slopes of Kiefer Valley, about two miles northwest of Altura. Federally endangered Karner blue butterflies can sometimes be seen on savanna patches north of the old town site of Beaver. Buried 40 years ago in a flash flood, the town and most of the valley lay in ruins after a century of abuse had left its forested hills clear-cut and its slopes grazed to the

ground. Today the valley is again rich in flora and fauna, a testament to committed conservation.

For birders, the Whitewater Valley is a warbler hot spot during spring migration; both bald and golden eagles soar above, and Louisiana waterthrushes flit about near clear, rushing streams. The spring-fed river and its tributaries contain, among other fish, native brook trout as well as introduced brown and rainbow trout. All together, some 49 species of mammals coexist in these units, and 237 species of birds appear in the area at one time or another.

At the northeast end of the wildlife management area is the town of Weaver, and north of it, off County Road 84 some two and a half miles out on the Mississippi River floodplain, lies the **Weaver Dunes Preserve Scientific and Natural Area❖.** A 697-acre swath of sand prairie edged with oak savanna, this unique river terrace habitat was formed from wind-blown sands and mud deposited over centuries by the an-

Swaths of scarlet sumac brighten Frontenac's autumnal landscape (left). Sumac provides a perch for the downy woodpecker (above); in winter this hardy resident forages fly larvae from plant galls.

cient Mississippi, Chippewa, and Zumbro rivers. Co-owned by the Nature Conservancy and the state, the property's starkly beautiful landscape features grassy swales, sheltered slopes, blowouts (sand hollows scooped out by the wind), dry ridges, and pockets of grassless shifting sand dunes, some up to 30 feet high. Among the many species that have adapted to these diverse habitats are the Ottoe skipper, a rare butterfly, and the very infrequently seen (in Minnesota) rough-seeded fameflower. Other unusual plants include clasping milkweed, wild indigo, and cliff goldenrod. For Blanding's turtle, a state-threatened species that nests in the sandy uplands and uses the extensive wetlands in the adjacent McCarthy Lake Wildlife Management Area, this site is one of the most important in the country. Weaver Dunes is rich in birdlife as well. In November the backwaters of the bottoms are bright with flocks of white tundra swans: More than 10,000 birds may visit in a typical year, and smaller concentrations gather in late March and early April.

LEFT: *Each spring streamsides and wet meadows in southern Minnesota turn a buttery yellow, painted by marsh marigolds, a bog-loving wildflower.*

RIGHT: *Prairie Creek spills over a watery limestone ledge at Hidden Falls in Nerstrand Big Woods State Park, a rare remnant of the hardwood forest that once blanketed the entire region.*

One of the state's premier birding spots, **Frontenac State Park❖,** lies some 30 miles upstream on the west side of Lake Pepin, a natural lake in the main channel of the Mississippi. Created by the delta that formed at the mouth of the Chippewa River (and now further maintained by a lock and dam at Alma), the lake—some 26 miles long and 2 miles wide—is one of the last refuges for the upper Mississippi River's population of paddlefish, evolutionary relics from before the age of dinosaurs. The spatula-snouted, scaleless fish were once fairly common here below Saint Anthony Falls, but overfishing and locks and dams blocking their traditional spawning grounds have drastically reduced their numbers.

The state park encloses a large-timbered floodplain forest backed by a bluff-top upland. An important stopover for northward migrating warblers, the forest is a major nesting area for the prothonotary warbler; above, hawks and eagles patrol the bluff top. More than 200 bird species visit this park every spring, and around the end of the first week in May warblers appear in large numbers. Other birds visiting the area include bald and golden eagles, ruddy turnstones, and sanderlings.

In the 1850s, as treaties with native tribes opened the interior to settlement, European immigrant farmers moving west of the Mississippi into Minnesota found a huge tract of unbroken forest dominated by immense sugar maples, basswoods, and red oaks. Cool and shaded, the interior of this forest was a cathedral-like place with little brushy understory except pockets of open wetlands in the low areas. Extending from near present-day Saint Cloud in the north to Mankato in the south, the forest covered some 3,000 square miles of south-central Minnesota. The settlers simply called it the Big Woods and began chopping it down to convert it into farmhouses, barns, towns, fields, and firewood. Today, less than 10 percent of the Big Woods remains, mostly as scattered remnants of upland forest and wetlands.

ABOVE: *In 1844 when John Casper Wild painted Fort Snelling at the confluence of the Mississippi and Minnesota rivers, settlers and fire had cleared the bluffs and valley; today forest has reclaimed the terrain.*

The finest surviving example of this ecosystem is **Nerstrand Big Woods State Park❖,** a 1,500-acre stand that miraculously escaped the clearing holocaust. Located about 10 miles northeast of Faribault on County Road 27, this impressive climax maple-basswood forest sustains a whole suite of now rare and threatened species of plants and animals. More than 50 varieties of wildflowers flourish here, as do many kinds of ferns and mushrooms. Wood's sedge (a small slender grass growing in deeply shaded forest) makes an appearance, along with increasingly uncommon wood thrushes, blue-winged and cerulean warblers, and delicate endangered dwarf trout lilies, southeast Minnesota's only true endemic plant species.

Nerstrand lies within the watershed of the **Cannon River,** which empties into the Mississippi just north of Red Wing. The name of the Cannon is an English corruption of the French *Rivière aux Canots,* or River of Canoes, because Dakota and French fur traders trekking up the valley frequently hid their canoes near the river's mouth. Historically the Cannon was a major east-west route for Native Americans; the Straight River, in the Cannon watershed, became a principal highway for European settlers headed west onto the prairies.

A portion of the Cannon, still a popular canoe river, has been designated a state wild and scenic river. The valley supports a rich assortment of wildlife, rare plants, mussel species, and endangered ecosystems. Some 28 rare plant species grow here, including the endemic dwarf trout lily, and 131 bird species, among them bald eagles, breed here as well. Small bluff prairies cling to south- and southwest-facing slopes, patches of tallgrass prairie dot the western highlands, and calcareous seepage fens occupy lower slopes in the Cannon River Wilderness Area, a county park.

A GRAND CONVERGENCE: THE SAINT PAUL–MINNEAPOLIS REGION

The distinctive features of the seven-county Minneapolis–Saint Paul metropolitan area—rolling hills, flat plains, deep river valleys, and chains of lakes—are the complex consequences of southbound ice fronts that stalled here some 14,000 years ago. This region lies at the center of some epochal natural convergences. Stretching north of the Twin Cities is a large, flat sand plain bounded on the east by the Saint Croix River, on the west by the Mississippi River, and on the south by the lake-strewn moraine upon which the cities stand. The moraine extends some 40 miles from the Wisconsin border to west of Lake Minnetonka.

The most obvious convergence here is the confluence of three of the state's four major rivers. The Minnesota slices into the moraine from the southwest, emptying into the Mississippi at Fort Snelling. The Mississippi flows in from the northwest, zigzags through the moraine, and exits to the southeast. From the north, the clear waters of the Saint Croix slice into the moraine some 35 miles east of the cities, joining the Mississippi's muddy stream at Prescott, Wisconsin.

Major conduits for glacial meltwater, the three waterways cut deeply into the moraine and through the Paleozoic sandstone and limestone bedrock. Today, a mere fraction of their size 11,000 years ago, the rivers flow through steep wooded valleys topped by buff-colored bluffs. Forested floodplain islands, sandbars, and sandy beaches characterize much of their bottomland. A large portion of the highly scenic shoreline and floodplain forest is now protected as municipal, county, and state parks and trails.

Fort Snelling offers a particularly dramatic view of the confluence of the Mississippi and Minnesota. Perched on a high river-cut rock terrace, this stone-walled 1824 frontier military outpost (now maintained as living museum) affords a commanding view of both rivers and their uplands and floodplain forested islands. The fort and the land below—which army officer and explorer Zebulon Pike purchased for the United States in 1805—are part of **Fort Snelling State Park❖** (off Route 5 near the Minneapolis–Saint Paul airport). The park also includes some fine calcareous seepage fens on lower slopes above the Minnesota River and some mesic oak savanna that is being maintained and improved with controlled burning. The park's floodplain forest provides birding in the spring; fine three-season canoeing, boating, hiking, and biking; and 18 miles of ski trails. An excellent year-round interpretive center on **Pike Island** below the fort presents a variety of interpretive programs explaining the rich natural and human history of the area. Outside, Bell's vireos flit about in the island's thickets.

The Twin Cities' morainic hills lie atop a Precambrian basin filled with sediments from successive Paleozoic seas. Beneath hundreds of feet of glacial debris is a network of prehistoric river-cut canyons and winding mesas that predate the glaciers by hundreds of millions of years. The only indications of their existence are the chains of lakes, which pooled on the debris that sank with the collapse of underlying glacial ice.

Descending from Lake Superior and the Canadian highlands, ice flowed into this ancient basin during the glacial era. At its southern rim, the glacier ran out of gas, dumping its load of red sands and clays across the east metropolitan area. The debris was high enough to partially deflect a later ice lobe advancing from the south and west, sparing the deep valleys and high bluffs to the south a certain burial.

North of the morainic hills lies the **Anoka sand plain**—really a series of coalescing sandy plains—where an ancient glacially diverted channel of the Mississippi once flowed. When European settlers arrived, they found a broad savanna of scrub oaks and dense scrub thickets pocked with sand blowouts and patches of shifting sand dunes. The landscape was maintained by drought and frequent fires, ignited by lightning or set by Native Americans to drive game. Poor soil though it was, the settlers determined to farm it. (An excellent place to view the major presettlement landscapes of Minnesota is the **Bell Museum of**

Natural History on the University of Minnesota's Minneapolis campus; the museum's dioramas are among the finest in the United States.)

Today most of the original landscape has been converted to sod farms, vegetable patches, and rapidly expanding urban development. Nonetheless, a few places still impart a sense of how this land probably looked 150 years ago. One is the **Helen Allison Savanna Scientific and Natural Area❖,** adjacent to the University of Minnesota's Cedar Creek Natural History Area, a large study site with a mixture of habitats about a mile east of the town of Bethel at the junction of County Roads 26 and 15. Named for writer and ecologist Helen Allison Irvine, this Nature Conservancy holding is perhaps the best tract of barrens oak savanna left in the region. Leased to the state, the SNA is a beautiful parklike dunescape supporting wet meadows in the swales. Maintained by controlled burns, more than 200 species of vascular plants thrive here. Rare species include the sea-beach needlegrass growing in sandy blowouts near the dune crests, which are rimmed with sand reed grass. Wet pockets contain state-endangered tall nut-rush, and arrow-leaved violets. Nearby Cedar Creek is an excellent birding area with species such as golden-winged warblers, alder flycatchers, and red-breasted nuthatches.

A sand-plain remnant with an entirely different look is **Uncas Dunes Scientific and Natural Area** in the **Sand Dunes State Forest❖.** (Access to the area is by gravel road, a left turn a half mile west of the intersection of County Routes 4 and 15, about five miles west of Zimmerman.) Offering an informative outdoor interpretative display, the site was named for the Uncas skipper, an uncommon butterfly of the central Great Plains that appears here, well east of its general range. The natural area is a scrub-oak savanna on a choppy, grass-covered dune field surrounded by shallow wetlands, wet meadows, fens, stunted oak woods, and alder swamp—a decidedly odd but pretty place. Two distinct kinds of sand prairie occur here, one on the crests of west- and south-facing dunes, the other on the cooler, moister north- and east-facing dunes.

The Lower Minnesota River Valley

From its head at Browns Valley near the South Dakota border, the trench that contains the Minnesota River runs like a slash across the face of southwestern Minnesota. At its bottom, the lilliputian river winds and

LEFT: *A white-tailed deer keeps watch among goldenrod and wavyleaf thistle. Exploding deer populations now threaten the survival of many rare woodland plants.*
RIGHT: *A stand of tall silver maples flourishes in the Minnesota Valley National Wildlife Refuge, where each year spring floods drown out the maple's dry-land competitors.*

twists and loops as if it has no idea what to do with the vast valley it has been given. Five miles wide at places and up to 250 feet deep, the valley was created when a prehistoric monster deluge called Glacial River Warren drained a giant body of meltwater, Glacial Lake Agassiz. The lake, trapped between a rock ledge at Browns Valley and the retreating wall of ice to the north, finally topped the barricade and unleashed its torrent down the lowland to the southeast.

Rising and falling as climates cooled and warmed, Warren eventually died when the retreating ice uncovered other drainages to the north that quickly siphoned off Agassiz's waters. A major route onto the western prairies for Native Americans, adventurers, military expeditions, fur traders, and settlers, the Minnesota Valley today supports an impressive mix of habitats and riverine wildlife.

Most of these can be experienced in the 42-mile stretch of river just above its confluence with the Mississippi where Warren sliced into the morainic hills and sedimentary bedrock underlying the Twin Cities. From the upstream end of Fort Snelling State Park to the town of Belle Plaine, substantial areas of the floodplain and shorelines are protected in a string of state, county, and municipal parks and trails, state scientific and natural areas, and federal holdings.

The primary federal presence in the region is the **Minnesota Valley National Wildlife Refuge❖,** which maintains several parcels. (Go south at the 34th Street exit of I-494 to refuge headquarters on East 80th Street.) Within the refuge, the river twists through steep wooded moraines, the residue of at least four glacial advances. The broad valley floor is laced with marshes, calcareous seepage fens, wet mead-

ABOVE: *An aquatic member of the weasel family, the mink is common in the Minnesota River valley; it subsists mainly on a diet of muskrat and is, in turn, a prey of the area's great horned owls, bobcat, and foxes.*

ows, bottomland forest, and here and there, both dry and wet prairie.

A well-developed trail system leads visitors into most of these areas, which protect a rich mix of habitats and wildlife. Some 50 different mammals live in the bottomlands, including 7 species of bats, beavers, muskrat, deer, badgers, weasels, and mink. About 260 species of birds, 32 of them tropical migrants, can be seen as well. Most important are the unusual number of uncommon, rare, and state-endangered species found along this lengthy stretch of river: eastern pipistrelle (a bat), eastern spotted skunk, Blanding's turtle, blue racer snakes, loggerhead shrikes, and Wilson's phalarope, among many others. A wide range of prairie plants flourish on rock outcrops, and calcareous seepage fens sustain specialized flora that have evolved to utilize the wet, high-calcium environment of the alkaline springs. Such plants include shrubby cinquefoil, bog birch, and small white lady's slippers.

Of the refuge's many special places, two are particularly appealing to birders and hikers: the **Bass Ponds,** a beautiful area south of refuge headquarters favored by warblers, and **Louisville Swamp,** a 2,400-acre mix of marsh, bottomland forest, and oak savanna at the intersection of Route 169 and 145th Street south of Shakopee. Trails wind through both areas.

West of the Minnesota valley south to Mankato, the land opens up

ABOVE: *A consummate swimmer, the fish-eating river otter inhabits many of the state's woodland streams and northern lakeshores. Slides in the snow or on riverbanks are often evidence of its playful presence.*

and flattens; trees disappear, and the sky seems enormous. This region was once the eastern edge of the tallgrass prairie, an amazing mosaic of grassland and wetland ecosystems that is hard to imagine today. In the swales grew wet prairie—stands of bulrush, sedges, and cordgrass that chattered in the wind. The uplands supported black-soil prairie, a grass-and-forb community dominated by big bluestem and Indian grass. On the stony moraines, on the pebble-rich river terraces, and among the bedrock outcrops were dry prairie, gravel prairie, and limestone prairie, each characterized by different suites of species. Low areas were dotted with small lakes and sloughs, which contained myriad streams. Great herds of elk and bison wandered the range, and a profusion of ducks and geese periodically darkened the skies. Mink, otters, beavers, and muskrat found homes along the larger rivers.

Today the wetlands are mostly drained or filled, and the prairie is planted in corn. Many of the rivers and streams have been converted to sluiceways, stripped of shoreline forest and wetlands and in many places actually straightened to carry off excess water more efficiently—and incidentally erode the soil. Yet despite the ravages of industrial society, vestiges of the former biological wealth here can still be found.

A few such places are the mouths of the Minnesota's principal tributaries where they spill into the river's enormous meltwater valley. Nine

47

Above: *With a stocky body, long neck, and wingspan of ten feet, the American white pelican is one of the continent's largest birds. Although it winters in the south, it breeds in northern areas such as Minnesota.*

major rivers flow into the Minnesota between Browns Valley and Mankato: from the north the **Pomme de Terre, Chippewa,** and **Hawk;** from the south the **Whetstone, Lac qui Parle, Yellow Medicine, Redwood, Cottonwood,** and **Blue Earth.** Forced to drop 200 to 250 feet to the valley floor over the course of a few miles, these streams have all cut deeply into the glacial clays on their final stretches. Some of these reaches feature big-bouldered rapids and narrow channels beneath high, forested bluffs—habitat for beavers, mink, red and gray foxes, hawks, turkey vultures, songbirds, woodpeckers, and many species of waterfowl. Other sections hold bass and walleye (many are stocked). Today most of these major confluences are protected state, county, or city parks. Noteworthy among them are **Minneopa State Park❖,** five miles west of Mankato; **Flandrau State Park❖,** at New Ulm; and **Alexander Ramsey City Park❖,** in Redwood Falls, a particularly scenic spot where the Redwood River tumbles over granite boulders through a landscape reminiscent of northern Minnesota.

At its maximum volume, Glacial River Warren sometimes slashed to the granitic foundation of the continent. A good place to see the result is **Upper Sioux Agency State Park❖** (southeast of Granite Falls on

ABOVE: *When geologist George Featherstonhaugh explored the broad Minnesota River valley in 1835, he reported that this narrow stretch near New Ulm was so pleasing that his party was "all in high spirits."*

Route 67), where the Yellow Medicine River twists and turns and tumbles to the valley floor through a steep wooded gorge laced with rapids and punctuated by beaver dams. A fine interpretative display at the park's visitor center explains the origin and natural history of the Minnesota River valley. In the early days of their brief but bloody six-week conflict with white rule in 1862, starving Dakota burned the Indian agency to the ground. The Dakota were subsequently expelled from the region, their treaty-sanctioned rights to the valley nullified.

Take nearby Route 23 north into Granite Falls to glimpse the scouring power of Glacial River Warren. As the highway descends into the river's legendary trench, the view down the valley presents a peculiar landscape of hummocks, knobs, dark ridges, and choppy terrain. **Granite Falls Memorial Park❖,** immediately east of the intersection of Routes 23 and 67, affords a good opportunity to explore. Once Warren's riverbed, the rocks are gneisses, composed of quartz, feldspar, biotite, and amphibolite melted together under tremendous heat and pressure. These cooked metamorphics—at 3.5 billion years old among the most ancient rocks on earth—have eroded at different rates and assumed varying shapes and structures.

THE UPPER MINNESOTA RIVER VALLEY

Some 13 miles up the river above Montevideo, the Minnesota River valley changes character. From a winding stream flowing between wooded banks, it opens into a delta marsh and then the first of four long, wide lakes separated by delta marshes. These river lakes were originally natural impoundments formed from silt and sand washed into the Minnesota by the waters of the Lac qui Parle, Pomme de Terre, Yellow Bank, and Whetstone rivers. Today, managed for flood control by the U.S. Army Corps of Engineers, they provide a wealth of habitat for waterfowl and other riparian species.

Lac qui Parle State Park❖ is on the delta of the Lac qui Parle River at the south end of Lac qui Parle Lake (the name is the French translation of the Dakotan "Lake Which Talks"). The park, which is off Route 33, lies within the **Lac qui Parle Wildlife Management Area❖,** extending 25 miles upstream to the dam just below the town of Odessa. The WMA is managed for a range of aquatic wildlife, chiefly game species such as ducks, geese, mink, muskrat, beavers, and pheasant. The best birding is at the south end of the lake.

Two fine prairie tracts grace the uplands here. Owned by the Nature Conservancy, 1,102-acre **Chippewa Prairie❖** occupies a level terrace above the Minnesota River valley floor about three miles north of Milan and two miles west of Route 59. The proliferation of rocks on the property—once the boulder-strewn shoreline of Glacial River Warren—spared it from the plow, if not from grazing cattle. Adjacent to the Lac qui Parle WMA, the prairie is an excellent example of a black-soil prairie dominated by six-foot-tall big bluestem, sprawling ground plum, and lavender-spiked dotted blazing star. Among the many other species abounding here are side-oats grama, prairie dropseed, soft lavender-colored pasqueflowers, and purple coneflowers. Short-eared owls can sometimes be seen drifting low over the flats, hunting mice and insects. The bluffs above the marshes on the western edge are a good vantage point for observing the flocks of ducks, geese, and shorebirds that migrate through in fall and spring.

RIGHT: *At the Big Stone National Wildlife Refuge, a sleek great egret poses motionless in shallow water. The stumps are the remains of a grove of floodplain trees—green ash, American elm, box elder, and silver maple.*

The other tract, also adjacent to the Lac qui Parle WMA, is **Plover Prairie❖.** On the south side of the river valley, the preserve is on a river terrace about four miles north of Bellingham and 1.5 mile east of Route 75. In this fine example of wet mesic prairie, bluejoint grass and prairie cordgrass, closed (bottle) gentian, and golden Alexanders grow among the shallow wetlands, bulrush marshes, and sedge meadows. Habitat here is ideal for resident upland plovers, marbled godwits, and many species of waterfowl.

For nine river miles along Route 7 above Marsh Lake, the Minnesota is an intimate stream again, a winding, wooded river. About a mile south of Odessa, above the artificial dam on Route 75, the river once again opens into a landscape of marsh, floodplain forest, flooded forest, prairie and grass uplands, and granite outcrops. This is the southern end of the **Big Stone National Wildlife Refuge❖,** an 11,355-acre parcel of river valley, managed principally for ducks and geese. However, a rich mix of habitats support a variety of nongame species as well. The wetlands, prairie tracts, and wooded areas along the south side of the river provide excellent birding opportunities, as does the refuge's auto tour. The floodplain forest is an important stopover for migrating warblers in the spring. In addition, the refuge contains some 1,700 acres of original prairie.

Bigstone Lake, above Ortonville, is the source of the Minnesota River and was formed by the silt and sand delta at the mouth of the Whetstone River. Habitats around the lake and on its islands range from floodplain forest and sand beach to upland grasslands and bluff prairies. On the north shore of the lake, **Big Stone Lake State Park❖** comprises two parcels along Route 7 on a lower terrace of the Warren trench. The northern parcel contains **Bonanza Prairie Scientific and Natural Area❖,** a fine example of undisturbed glacial-till hill prairie. Bonanza is a mixture of dry and black-soil prairie along with bur-oak savanna running up a steep side wall of the trench above Big Stone Lake. The well-drained, gravelly soil here supports a mix of prairie species. Among many species growing on the drier uplands are purple coneflowers, purple prairie clover, little bluestem, Flodman's thistle, and dotted blazing star, while big bluestem and Indian grass inhabit the moister slopes. The state-endangered prairie moonwort (a fern) and rare Missouri milk vetch also grow on this tract.

Visitors driving north and west on Routes 7 and 28 toward Browns Valley finally top the Big Stone Moraine—the natural dam that impounded Glacial Lake Agassiz. Both spectacular and informative, the view here encompasses the entire head of the Minnesota River valley, as well as the morainic hills that for so many years held back Agassiz's waters. Terraces mark the levels that the glacial stream cut as it gouged its way through rock debris and ultimately the bedrock below. The boulders scattered about withstood the force of the river.

Given the cataclysmic geologic event that occurred here some 11,000 years ago, **Traverse Gap,** just north of Browns Valley, is almost astonishing in its insignificance. Visitors driving across it on Minnesota Route 28 and South Dakota Route 10 find themselves in a shallow depression among low hills. North of the road is Lake Traverse, the headwaters of the north-flowing Red River of the North. To the south, the road's shoulder drops away into a swampy, floodplain forest, the headwaters of the south-flowing Minnesota River. It is difficult to see this spot as an important divide, let alone picture the torrent unleashed when Agassiz broke through the barricade that stood here.

MINNESOTA'S SOUTHWESTERN CORNER: THE PRAIRIE COTEAU

In the extreme southwest portion of the state is a height of land that testifies to the immense forces that shaped this region. The range of steep hills running roughly from the Florida River on the South Dakota line to the Iowa border south of Jackson is the eastern edge of a bedrock highland known as Coteau de Prairies or **Prairie Coteau.**

Shaped like a flatiron, the Coteau's prow juts into southeast North Dakota, its high eastern edge running south through Minnesota well into Iowa, and its lower western flank extending down through eastern South Dakota. Rising more than 750 feet above the surrounding plain at its high northern end, the Coteau rests on a mass of hard quartzite— the uplifted fossil floor of an ancient sea. The plateau was formed from debris left by successive sheets of ice far older than the encircling ter-

OVERLEAF: *At Hole-in-the-Mountain Prairie, native wildflowers and big bluestem grasses take on the color of the setting sun. Of the state's original 18 million acres of prairie, a mere 150,000 acres now remain.*

ABOVE: *Yellow prairie coneflowers bloom at Hole-in-the-Mountain Prairie, a rare botanical pocket harboring hundreds of flowering species.*

rain, and during the last glacial advance, the wedge of the Coteau split the glacial mass, forcing the ice sheet down its flanks. The steep hills in this region are the stream-dissected debris left by that last ice sheet, which crested but did not cover the highland.

Known locally as **Buffalo Ridge,** the highlands of the Prairie Coteau today divide two of the continent's major drainage basins. Water flowing off the western flank of the moraine runs eventually to the Missouri River, while that on the eastern side goes to the Mississippi. The headwaters of a number of the region's most significant rivers can be found among the rolling hills: the Rock and Flandreau on the west side of the ridge; the Des Moines, Whetstone, Lac qui Parle, Yellow Medicine, Redwood, and Cottonwood on the east.

Amid this stream-dissected landscape are two excellent prairie remnants south and west of the little town of Florence at the junction of Routes 23 and 14. **Prairie Coteau Scientific and Natural Area❖,** some 12 miles south on Route 23, is a 329-acre tract of hill prairie near Holland maintained by the Minnesota Department of Natural Resources. The dry prairie on the upland is dominated by little bluestem, side-oats grama, prairie dropseed, and many species found in the mixed-grass

ABOVE: *Among the bluestem, a pair of dragonflies finds a purple prairie clover; thousands of insect species inhabit a typical prairie remnant.*

prairie of the Dakotas. The wet prairie in the lowlands features bluejoint and northern reed grass. Rare Dakota and Ottoe skippers, both prairie butterflies, are found here as well. Brilliantly colored prairie flowers grow profusely: Yellow-headed puccoons, lavender prairie smoke, red blazing stars, purple New England asters, pale red prairie phlox, and a host of others provide a continuous bloom throughout the season.

Another example of a hill prairie, **Hole-in-the-Mountain Prairie**❖ lies above Flandreau Creek about 1.5 miles south of Lake Benton on Route 75. (This 775-acre Nature Conservancy property is part of a 4,300-acre prairie tract that begins south of Lake Benton and runs along the west and east side of 75 toward the Altona State Wildlife Management Area.) At Hole-in-the-Mountain, tallgrass prairie has given way to the mixed grasses of the drier plains to the west. Side-oats grama, needlegrass, and western wheatgrass are among some 60 species of grasses, sedge, and rush the area supports, as well as 200 species of wildflowers and 25 species of butterflies, including Dakota, Ottoe, and Pawnee skippers.

Two other sites in this area are worth visiting. About 16 miles south of Hole-in-the-Mountain on Route 75, the legendary pipestone quarries of the Plains Indians are now federally protected and maintained as the

LEFT: *Because prairie flowers bloom at different times, they do not compete for vital insect pollinators; here a monarch butterfly feeds on goldenrod.*
RIGHT: *Once the sandy bottom of an ancient sea, this quartzite ridge at Blue Mounds State Park, with its dramatic view of the green rolling plains below, is part of Minnesota's Prairie Coteau.*

Pipestone National Monument❖. In a low trough along the western edge of Buffalo Ridge, the quarries lie within a long, low outcrop of sheet quartzite, sandstone cooked and chemically hardened under great pressure into rock slabs almost marblelike in appearance.

Known as Sioux quartzite, the rock originated in the sandy bottom of a shallow sea that stood here some 1.4 billion years ago. Characteristically laced with iron oxides, the quartzite is usually a pretty pink but can range from white to deep reddish purple. The pipestone is a thin layer of red siltstone within the harder quartzite. (This siltstone's official name is Catlinite for the noted American artist George Catlin, whose paintings of nineteenth-century Native American life first brought these quarries to the world's attention.) Pipestone is sacred to many Plains tribes, and Native Americans have long carved their ceremonial pipes from it. The monument's excellent visitor center offers much more background information.

Some 16 miles south of the town of Pipestone on Route 75, **Blue Mounds State Park❖** encloses an attractive 1,500-acre tract of damaged prairie and grassland. Located in a high area untouched by the last glaciation, the park straddles a peculiar—and beautiful—landscape of slightly rolling rangeland littered with quartzite outcrops. Because of the rocky terrain, the park and much of the surrounding countryside escaped the ravages of the plow. A 1.5-mile, east-facing scarp of Sioux quartzite, the geologic centerpiece of the park, drops off precipitously along much of its length, plunging 90 feet in some places. To settlers heading west, the highland appeared from a distance as a blue-tinted mound rising out of the surrounding plain, hence its name. An ongoing prairie restoration program includes the reintroduction of bison; the herd now numbers more than 30 animals.

WESTERN MINNESOTA:
HARDWOOD HILLS TO NORTHERN PRAIRIES

The two landforms that define the landscape of western Minnesota are hard to miss. One is the absolutely flat valley of the Red River of the North, and the other is the range of high wooded hills that trace the valley nearly the entire length of its eastern side. This valley occupies the ancient lake bed of Glacial Lake Agassiz, the huge body of water that covered much of northwestern Minnesota some 10,000 years ago. When European settlers reached this region 150 years ago, they encountered a sea of tallgrass prairie interspersed with vast swaths of wet prairie, bluejoint, cordgrass, and sedge meadows.

Glaciers deposited the jumbled hills to the east, a series of lateral and end moraines that lie alongside and atop one another. More than 1,500 feet above sea level and 500 feet above the plain to the west, these high, rugged hills stopped the fires that regularly swept in from the west, enabling thick forests to blanket the upper slopes. Along the western fringe of the hills runs a narrow band of oak woodland and savanna—an intermediate ecotone separating prairie and woodland—that once extended in various forms from here to Texas.

Life on these west-facing hills had to adapt to naturally occurring or human-set fires that constantly came off the prairie. Repeated cycles of fire confined more easterly species such as maples, basswoods, elms,

LEFT: *Immense, mercurial, and compelling: The overarching prairie sky is as important to the western landscape as the land itself. Here the sun sets spectacularly over Minnesota's Glacial Lakes State Park.*

and ashes, as well as woody underbrush, to protected pockets (usually gorges or ravines) or areas east of such natural firebreaks as streams and lakes. Only tough-skinned bur oaks could withstand these grass fires, and even today this species dominates many forests along the transitional line.

More than 11,000 years ago, Glacial Lake Agassiz broke through a moraine at its southern end near the present-day town of Browns Valley, and its water level dropped. As the climate fluctuated between cool and warm, Agassiz's level rose and fell. Old shorelines, called strandlines, can still be observed, especially on the eastern shore. For centuries these gravel-packed ridges, running parallel to one another all up and down the valley, were highways for Native Americans. During early European settlement they were followed by oxcart caravans that hauled furs and other trade goods between Pembina, in the northeastern corner of North Dakota, and the southern settlements around Saint Paul—a transportation system soon put out of business by the steamboat and the advent of the railroad.

After visiting the hills and lakes northwest of the Twin Cities near Sauk Centre, this chapter's itinerary proceeds north via Inspiration Peak to Pelican Rapids. It then jogs eastward, crossing three biological zones on a single stretch of highway, to explore Itasca State Park, where the Mississippi River begins its nearly 2,500-mile journey to the Gulf of Mexico. A visit to the northern prairie remnants southeast of Crookston, in the state's far northwestern corner, concludes the journey.

THE GREAT TRANSITION:
THE WESTERN PRAIRIES AND THE HARDWOOD HILLS

Northwest of Minneapolis lies a wooded land of high hills dotted with countless lakes. This rolling lake-strewn landscape represents the tracks of glaciers and was the dumping ground of at least four different ice advances from the west, north, and east. A major topographic high point in the state, these hills once supported extensive patches of tallgrass prairie, as well as mixed forests of basswood, oak, sugar

---

OVERLEAF: *At Itasca State Park, tamarack trees shade still waters, and sunlit boulders edge a rippling stream. From this idyllic source in central Minnesota flow the headwaters of the majestic Mississippi River.*

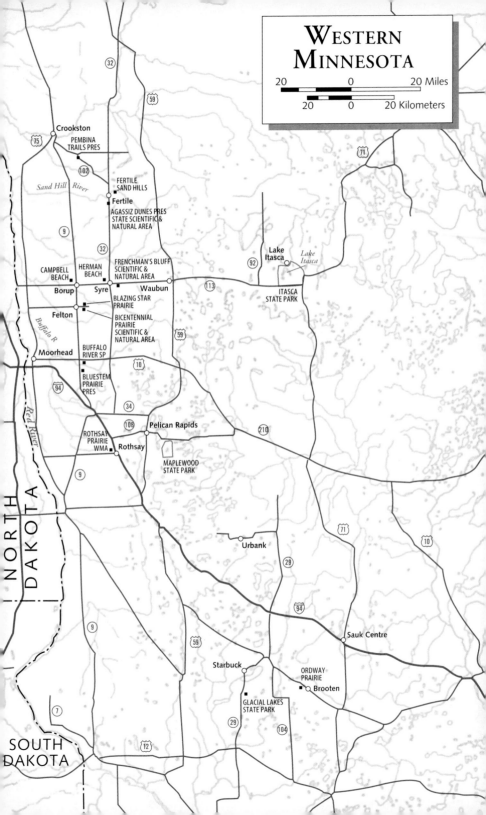

20 0 20 Miles
20 0 20 Kilometers

Crookston
PEMBINA TRAILS PRES
Sand Hill River
FERTILE SAND HILLS
Fertile
AGASSIZ DUNES PRES STATE SCIENTIFIC & NATURAL AREA
Lake Itasca
Lake Itasca
CAMPBELL BEACH
HERMAN BEACH
FRENCHMAN'S BLUFF SCIENTIFIC & NATURAL AREA
ITASCA STATE PARK
Borup
Syre
Waubun
BLAZING STAR PRAIRIE
Felton
Buffalo R
BICENTENNIAL PRAIRIE SCIENTIFIC & NATURAL AREA
Moorhead
BUFFALO RIVER SP
BLUESTEM PRAIRIE PRES
Red River
ROTHSAY PRAIRIE WMA
Rothsay
Pelican Rapids
MAPLEWOOD STATE PARK
NORTH DAKOTA
Urbank
Sauk Centre
SOUTH DAKOTA
Starbuck
ORDWAY PRAIRIE
Brooten
GLACIAL LAKES STATE PARK

maple, ash, hickory, and other hardwoods. Although much of it has been altered by subdivisions and farms, this landscape riddled with lakes, streams, kettle-hole ponds, marshes, and pretty valleys invites visitors to leave the interstate and explore.

Amid a particularly high and rolling region of this upland is **Ordway Prairie❖,** a 582-acre Nature Conservancy preserve that encompasses a rich mosaic of prairie habitats. Located southwest of Sauk Centre on Route 104 near the town of Brooten, the preserve lies at the woodland edge of the transition zone between former tallgrass prairie to the west and hardwood forests to the east.

Prairie fires periodically sweeping out of the west kept these steep, high-shouldered hills largely treeless. Today the lowlands shelter ponds, marshes, wet prairie, and flooded copses of willow and poplar. Dry gravel prairie extends along the upper slopes and hilltops, and calcareous fens—wet, soggy areas fed by calcium-carbonate–rich seeps that percolate out of the ground—are scattered along the lower slopes. A unique habitat, the fens support a range of uncommon species such as false asphodel, bog birch, and hairlike beak rush.

A few miles west on the same moraine lies another remnant landscape from the Pleistocene. South of Starbuck on Route 41, **Glacial Lakes State Park❖** is a 1,880-acre highland of steep grass-covered hills, wooded hollows, marshes, kettle-hole lakes, and kames. Composed of stratified sand and gravel, kames are created when glacial debris carried by meltwater pours into depressions on the ice surface. When the ice melts, these deposits form hills. Kettles are depressions left by melting ice blocks buried under glacial debris. As the ice blocks melt, the overlying debris collapses, and the resulting hole often fills with water.

This park also lies along the fire-maintained transition zone between western prairie and eastern woodlands. Historically, fires from the prairie climbed these hills with enough frequency and intensity to clear out all woody plants except thick-barked, fire-tolerant bur oaks, which are still dominant today. Although the property that became this park was once farmed, native prairie endures in some areas. In the spring solitary heads of pale blue and white pasqueflowers, a grassland plant, are among the first to show their colors, often even before the last of the snow has gone. Prairie clover, bluestems, Indian grass, wolfberry, and coneflowers bloom in turn on the grassy uplands. Coyotes roam

ABOVE: *When Plains Indians set annual fires to drive game—an event documented by George Catlin in his 1832 oil sketch* Prairie Meadows Burning*—the flames inadvertently maintained the prairie's complex ecosystem.*

the hills, home too for deer, beavers, and wood ducks. Hiking and bridle trails wind through the highland and hollows, and in winter visitors enjoy cross-country skiing, snowshoeing, and snowmobiling.

"Like sequins fallen on an old paisley shawl" wrote native son Sinclair Lewis to describe the lakes he saw from the bald summit of **Inspiration Peak❖.** The site, on County Route 38 west of Urbank, is about 45 miles northwest of Sauk Centre, the author's hometown, which became the model for Main Street's Gopher Prairie, the embodiment of claustrophobic small-town America. Actually a high kame, the peak sits atop the zenith of the Alexandria moraine, one of the state's highest and best-known glacial features. The lower slopes are cloaked in oak forest, and the crest is open bluff prairie. The view from the top is impressive: Rolling hills, woods, lakes, and fields extend in all directions. To the west, hardwood forest gives way to what was once open prairie. Here, with a little imagination, visitors can sense the enormity of the ice sheet that sculpted this landscape.

Above: *Glacial footprints pattern Glacial Lakes State Park, whose round, deep kettle lakes began when large blocks of buried ice melted; the debris on top then collapsed and the resulting cavity filled with water.*

One of the larger slices of this wood-and-grassland terrain lies about 35 miles northwest of Inspiration Peak. Encompassing 9,000 acres, **Maplewood State Park❖** (about seven miles east of Pelican Rapids on Route 108) contains numerous glacial features. Several kames can be explored on foot, but the centerpiece of the park is some 50 kettle lakes of varying sizes, shapes, and depths. This ruggedly beautiful terrain is almost a textbook example of stagnation moraine country. Here a glacial front came to a halt while the debris-loaded ice behind it kept flowing forward, creating huge piles of rock, gravel, soils, and sand.

Because the park is positioned at the very edge of the prairie-forest boundary, plant species common to both western prairie and eastern woodland are found here, as is vegetation from the transitional oak-savanna landscape that once stood between them. Very few prairie plants remain, intermixed with stands of bur oak. Basswood, sugar maple, elm, ash, and oak climb the north and east sides of the hills.

The Northern Prairies

Maplewood State Park occupies the boundary of the Alexandria moraine. Barely 15 miles west is land that was once wide, flat, open prairie. Stretching across the floor of Glacial Lake Agassiz, the luxuri-

ABOVE: *This cone-shaped hill at Glacial Lakes, a kame, was created when silt-laden waters from the surface of a melting glacier poured into a hole in the ice, gradually building up this tapered pile of debris.*

ous tallgrass prairie that grew here was long ago supplanted by wheat and barley. But the 4,000-acre **Rothsay Prairie Wildlife Management Area❖,** about four miles west of the town of Rothsay off County Route 26, was fortuitously spared the plow because the prairie here is a mosaic of fens, marshes, and wet meadows. Big bluestem, marsh muhly, and a variety of sedges thrive in and around the fens. Cold seeps loaded with calcium carbonate have created mini-peatlands here. Wet meadows support sedges, rushes, prairie cordgrass, and bluejoint while cattails, hardstem bulrushes, and great reed grass stand along the marshes. A great birding area, Rothsay attracts prairie falcons and yellow rail, both rare in the state.

The featured performers here, however, are greater prairie chickens. Once numerous throughout the tallgrass prairie in southern and western Minnesota, these members of the grouse family provided both Native Americans and early European settlers with a steady source of protein. Thriving on an equal mix of grassland and cropland, the birds actually increased their range during early European settlement. But as grassland, their traditional breeding grounds, continued to be eliminated and market hunting expanded, the species quickly declined. By the early 1930s the prairie chicken was barely hanging on. Granted state

ABOVE: *Each spring greater prairie chickens return to their traditional display grounds, or leks, where males—leaping, fluttering, and "booming"—try to impress watching females with an ancient mating dance.*

protection in 1935, the birds, now scattered through the remnant western prairies, number only about 3,000 today.

Greater prairie chickens are unquestionably one of the more spectacular prairie species, principally because of their bizarre courtship antics. Around the end of March, often while snow is still on the ground, as many as 40 males gather at a certain site, generally a short-grass or grazed area. Here they fight and display for positions near the center of the arena, also called the booming ground for the peculiar kettledrum-like noise the males make in full display. Audible up to a mile away, these sounds issue from an inflated pair of bright orange skin sacs near the base of the cocks' necks that serve as resonating chambers. Their territories established, the birds erect their pinnae (stiff tufts of neck feathers) fan their tails, spread their wings, and stamp their feet in a calculated effort to attract the hens. Mating is generally accomplished by the cocks occupying the center territories. The males perform for several hours in the morning, beginning just before daybreak, and again at dusk. Peak time to see them is April through mid-May.

Unlike the homogeneous agricultural landscape they have become in the twentieth century, the prairies were once a rich, complex mix of plant and animal communities that varied depending on local conditions. Some 25 miles north of Rothsay is a prairie of a different kind. **Bluestem Prairie Scientific and Natural Area**❖ (1,296 acres of which are leased by the state from a 3,258-acre holding of the Nature Conservancy) abuts the southern edge of Buffalo River State Park, about 15 miles east of Moorhead south of the junction of Routes 10 and 9. The northern tallgrass prairie here is one of the largest high-quality remnants in the Midwest. Extending along several ancient beach lines of Glacial Lake Agassiz, the giant pool of meltwater that stood here some 10,000 years ago, the mix of prairie includes wet prairie and sedge meadows in the lowland, black-soil prairie on the drier ground, dry prairie on the ridgelines, and calcareous fen along the ridge slopes. More than 300 species of native plants—including 54 native grasses—are found here, as well as a number of rare plants and animals. Particularly unusual are false asphodel and small white lady's slippers; regal fritillary and Dakota skipper butterflies; mouselike prairie voles; and Henslow's sparrows, upland sandpipers, marbled godwits, and greater prairie chickens—in all, 70 kinds of birds and 20 butterfly species.

A wooded island in a sea of agriculture, **Buffalo River State Park**❖ (on Route 10 east of Moorhead) straddles the Buffalo River, an eastern tributary of the Red River. The moist bottomland supports a healthy floodplain forest of elm, ash, cottonwood, and basswood, and the conjunction of forest and prairie offers a chance to see wildlife of both environments. Among the variety of woodland creatures thriving here are beavers, four species of woodpeckers, vireos, phoebes, and a number of woodland warblers. More than 200 species of birds visit this scenic park at one time or another during the year.

A number of other prairie remnants cluster in this corner of Minnesota. Occurring on or between old Agassiz strandlines, these areas were either too stony to accommodate livestock or too inconvenient to plow. An impressive 6,000-acre collection of prairie lands extends some 10 miles north of the Buffalo River, including the **Felton Prairie Scientific and Natural Area**❖, a 1,500-acre complex protected by the state, coun-

---

OVERLEAF: *Prairie blazing star takes center stage at Bluestem Prairie. Although the magenta-flowered plant grows only 30 inches high, its vigorous roots can descend up to 16 feet into the prairie's biomass.*

LEFT: *Fierce fighters and solitary hunters, raccoons are native to the Americas. They spend their nights foraging along woodland streams, such as those in Buffalo River State Park, for small mammals, berries, nuts, insects, and fish.*

RIGHT: *The Buffalo River winds through the park's lush floodplain forest on its way to the Red River. European settlers named the watercourse for the bison that wintered along one of its southern tributaries.*

ty, and the Nature Conservancy. **Blazing Star Prairie,** a unit of Felton, lies about four miles east of the town of Felton on County Route 34. (**Bicentennial Prairie,** another unit of Felton, is adjacent to Blazing Star on the southwest.) A combination of wet, gravel, and black-soil prairie, Blazing Star contains a number of rare and state-endangered species of native plants and animals. Blazing Star helps protect four prairie-chicken booming grounds located within a two-mile radius of the tract. Among the unusual avian species observed here are Baird's sparrows and chestnut-collared longspurs, also seen on the adjacent B-Bar-B Ranch. The best times to visit this site are early spring, when pinkish prairie smoke and white and purple pasqueflowers are in full bloom, and late summer, when magenta blazing stars, blue and white asters, and bright yellow sunflowers are splashed across the landscape.

ITASCA STATE PARK: JEWEL OF MINNESOTA PARKS

The convergence of three of the continent's major biomes—prairie, deciduous forest, and coniferous forest—in one mountainless state is unusual, so the opportunity to experience them all in a one-hour drive should not be missed. In addition to the three biomes, the 68 miles across Route 113 from the town of Borup east to Itasca State Park traverse the narrow prairie-forest transition zone that bisects the continent from Minnesota to Texas.

During the trip, visitors cross several strandlines of Glacial Lake Agassiz. The strands—ridges formed by wave action during long periods when lake levels were stable—appear as low rises on the flat plain. The higher the rise, the longer the lake stood at that particular level. One of the largest strandlines, the Campbell beach, straddles the highway about five and a half miles east of Borup; five more beaches appear before the town of Syre, where the highest, Herman beach, lies two and a half miles west of the intersection with Route 32.

A mile and a half east of Syre, the road begins to climb into moraine country. The hills here and to the north are part of a range that stretches south to Browns Valley, where a natural divide blocked Agassiz's drainage to the south, thus creating the big lake. Known as the Big Stone moraine, these hills are actually a huge, nearly continuous pile of debris left when the stagnating ice front of the last glacier melted. A little over a mile north of Route 113 on County Route 36, **Frenchman's Bluff Scientific and Natural Area❖**—named for a French pioneer family who settled here and mysteriously disappeared during a time of Indian-settler unrest—occupies a prominent glacially deposited hill atop the moraine. Standing 200 feet above the highest beach ridge, the bluff commands a panoramic view of the Big Stone moraine to the north and south—a line of low rolling hills cloaked in woods and fields stretching from horizon to horizon. Atop the bluff are a small prairie and a number of rare plants and animals.

West of Waubun, the terrain suddenly becomes steeper and forested as Route 113 climbs higher onto the moraine. Bur oaks and open fields give way to a landscape of aspens, maples, basswoods, elms, and green ashes. Within a few miles, these woods change in turn to a

forest increasingly dominated by aspens, birches, and evergreens. In less than 20 miles visitors have traversed four major ecosystems: tallgrass prairie, the oak-savanna prairie-to-forest transition zone, eastern deciduous forest, and northern coniferous forest. In the nineteenth century, before Europeans altered and homogenized these landscapes, the transitions were even more pronounced: pure prairie in the west and magnificent old-growth pinelands and hardwood forest in the east.

ABOVE: *After breeding in the North, the red-breasted merganser migrates through Minnesota, feeding in its many lakes and ponds.*
RIGHT: *Schoolcraft Island rises above a misty Lake Itasca. In 1832, explorer Henry Schoolcraft renamed the lake, once called Lac la Biche (Doe Lake) by voyageurs.*

Although the mixed landscape of northern hardwoods and pine that once blanketed these northern hills is now vastly altered, a superb remnant flourishes at the eastern end of Route 113 in 32,000-acre **Itasca State Park**❖ (the entrance is three miles north on Route 71). The park's principal lake, Itasca, is the purported headwaters of the Mississippi River, which flows north from the lake as a clean, bubbling stream and arrives 2,552 miles later at its wide polluted, silt-loaded mouth on the Gulf of Mexico. In truth, however, the Mississippi's headwaters are the myriad streams that flow into Lake Itasca from higher elevations.

The lake was named in 1832 by explorer Henry Schoolcraft, who was led there by an Ojibwa guide called OzaWindib. A self-taught geologist and ethnologist with a fanciful imagination, Schoolcraft coined

the name Itasca by combining the Latin words *veritas caput* ("true head") and lopping off the first and last three letters. He also created a legend about the lake, which he ascribed to the Ojibwa. Basically a re-tooled version of the Greek myth of Persephone starring the "noble red man," the concoction was later immortalized in Henry Wadsworth Longfellow's epic poem *Song of Hiawatha*.

The park lies within the hilly knob-and-kettle region of a moraine that preceded by several thousand years the glacial advance that deposited the wooded hills to the west. This earlier glacier left behind a variety of features now within the park: kames, kettle lakes, dry hollows, and an esker—a long, sinuous ridge of stratified glacial debris deposited by a river of meltwater that once flowed under the ice mass.

The park shelters a rich mix of ecological communities—marshes, bogs, northern hardwood forest, and remnant stands of old-growth red and white pine. In all, 24 hiking and biking trails meander through this century-old preserve, which also includes some four square miles of wild lands without paths. One such area is **Itasca Wilderness Sanctuary Scientific and Natural Area,** a 2,000-acre virgin forest that contains the state's largest single intact stand of red and white pine—a powerful reminder of the majestic trees that once covered much of northern Minnesota. In the forest's cathedral-like interior stand venerable giants, 250-to-300-year-old trees, whose preservation was a principal reason for creating the park. These trees are the sole survivors of a magnificent old-growth pine forest that was leveled by timber speculators at the end of the nineteenth century.

THE NORTHWEST CORNER: DELTAS, DUNE FIELDS, AND SAND HILLS

Along the ancient beaches and strandlines of Glacial Lake Agassiz's eastern perimeter is a starkly beautiful place where sandy rolling hills of grass and woods encompass the winding Sand Hill River. Stretching west and south of the town of Fertile, this rare combination of oak-sa-

LEFT: *The diversified forests of Itasca State Park include (clockwise from upper left) old-growth red and white pines, a remnant stand from a once-great northland pinery; a spruce tree in a forest bog, festooned with old man's beard moss; a lone, flaming sugar maple on an aspen-birch highland; and yellowing autumnal tamaracks along a marsh.*

vanna and dry-sand prairie is actually an extensive dune field formed from a sand delta laid down by the ancestor of the current river. The 640-acre municipally owned **Fertile Sand Hills❖** just west of town (self-guided tours are available) form its northern border, and the 434-acre **Agassiz Dunes Scientific and Natural Area❖,** a couple of miles southwest, anchors the south.

Considerably wider and wilder than the present-day Sand Hill and fed by a glacial lake behind a moraine to the northeast, the river that laid down this sand delta coursed west through the hills for more than 400 years. As it emptied its load of sand and silt into giant Lake Agassiz, the heavier sediments settled in an ever-thickening sand delta along Agassiz's eastern shore. When the lake's waters receded, they left this delta high and dry. An extended warm, arid period between 8,000 and 4,000 years ago dessicated the ecosystem here—probably a white spruce forest. Stripped of vegetation, the delta became an active dunescape, worked and reworked by the wind until cooler, moister times enabled plants to return, stabilizing the dunes.

In these sharply rolling, choppy hills, scattered clumps of stunted bur oak populate the grassy, south-facing slopes, aspens fill in the low hollows, and birch trees grow along the north-facing slopes. Active sand blowouts support creeping juniper and dry-sand prairie grasses and sedges. Prairie forbs and wildflowers abound, among them pasqueflower, bearberry, shell-leaf penstemon, dotted blazing star, and a host of others. Rare plants and animals include lark sparrows, greater prairie chickens, upland sandpipers, Indian rice grass, rush pink, and bent grass.

Northwest, between the towns of Fertile and Crookston, lie a cluster of scientific and natural areas and state wildlife management areas that protect several thousand acres of fine northern tallgrass prairie. The largest is the **Pembina Trails Preserve Scientific and Natural Area❖,** co-owned by the Nature Conservancy and the state. (From Fertile take Route 102 north, then County Route 45 east 6.5 miles.) Together these areas encompass 2,320 acres of extremely diverse prairie habitat lying across several of Agassiz's wave-cut strandlines. A ridge-and-swale topography supports black-soil prairie, wet prairie, gravel prairie sedge meadows, marsh, aspen woods, and old farm fields. Small calcareous fens line the sides of some of the low, sandy ridges.

ABOVE: *As much a part of the tallgrass prairie as the grasses themselves, sandhill cranes have for millennia nested on prairie wetlands such as these on the Pembina preserve in northwestern Minnesota.*

Here a number of rare and uncommon (in these parts) birds can be seen or heard, including nesting sandhill cranes, marbled godwits, rare yellow rail, Wilson's phalaropes, short-eared owls, and greater prairie chickens. Northern harriers can be seen beating over the low prairie ridges, while moose forage in the wet areas. Among the 196 native plants that occur naturally are a number of unusual species such as the hairlike beak rush, marsh arrow-grass, and false asphodel. The best time to visit these rolling northern reaches of Minnesota is late summer, when asters, sunflowers, blazing stars, and goldenrods paint the prairies red, white, lavender, blue, purple, and gold.

CHAPTER THREE

EASTERN MINNESOTA:
SAINT CROIX VALLEY TO THE NORTH SHORE

D ensely forested eastern Minnesota, from the mouth of the Saint Croix River near the Twin Cities north to Lake Superior and the Pigeon River on the Canadian border, is a region of considerable beauty, as well as ecological and geologic significance. Through its center runs the transition between two of North America's major forest biomes—deciduous forest of the south and boreal conifer forest—a still-discernible ecological segue that has been vastly altered in the aftermath of intensive logging and agriculture.

Forming Minnesota's eastern border with Wisconsin, the highly scenic valley of the Saint Croix River was carved by meltwater spilling from a huge glacial lake, a precursor of Lake Superior, some 11,000 years ago. Rich in wildlife, these forested lands became the traditional hunting grounds of the Dakota and a mecca for early European trappers. During the 1700s, the Dakota waged a fierce but losing war against invading Ojibwa driven into the region by expanding European settlement to the east. For the Ojibwa, the victory was short-lived. In 1837, under intense pressure from the territorial government, they signed the first of several treaties with the U.S. government that effectively opened these lands to settlement and unrestrained exploitation.

Once most of the coniferous forest here and elsewhere across northeastern Minnesota was dominated by great stands of white and

LEFT: *At Tettegouche State Park on the North Shore of Lake Superior, the rising sun tints the basalt cliffs a rusty red. Lucky birders may spot rare peregrine falcons soaring and hunting along this rocky coast.*

83

red pine. When big-time logging began in the early 1840s, the great pinery in the Saint Croix Valley was the first to go. Some 70 years later, the rest of the state had been cut clean as well.

Central to Minnesota's northeastern landscape are the waters of Lake Superior, the big lake's rugged, rockbound North Shore, and a series of thundering cataracts that tumble to the lake from the wild, densely forested highland above. Millennial events are still clearly visible in the Superior basin. The dark basalts that stand exposed along the shoreline and the meltwater-cut gorges of the Saint Croix Valley to the south are billion-year-old lava flows. Routed out by ice, the Superior basin was the birthplace of numerous glaciers that pushed south and east, transforming the face of the region.

This chapter begins near the Twin Cities in the lower Saint Croix River valley and follows the river north. After crossing the Kettle, a northern tributary of the upper Saint Croix, it angles northeast to Duluth and then traces Lake Superior's incredibly beautiful North Shore to Grand Portage and the Pigeon River.

THE VALLEY OF THE SAINT CROIX RIVER

About 10,000 years ago, in the dying days of the last glacial era, a mountain of ice that had lain for millennia in the Superior basin began its final meltdown. Seeking a natural outlet, the rising meltwater found its way into a natural lowland to the south. As it crashed down the valley, the gravel-laden water cut a steep channel that today contains one of the prettiest rivers in the region, the Saint Croix.

Flowing from headwaters in Solon Springs, Wisconsin, the **Saint Croix River** forms the Minnesota-Wisconsin border about 6 miles north of Danbury, Wisconsin, and begins its 140-mile run to its confluence with the Mississippi. On the way, it passes by seven state parks, three state forests, and four wildlife management areas. One of the original rivers in the National Wild and Scenic Rivers System, the Saint Croix and its tributary, the Namekagon, are today managed by the National Park Service as the **Saint Croix National Scenic Riverway❖.**

OVERLEAF: *A leaf-spattered forest road winds through an autumnal woodland of maple, aspen, and spruce just off the Caribou Trail, one of several routes into the vast reaches of Superior National Forest.*

CANADA

Pigeon River

Fort Charlotte

GRAND PORTAGE NAT MON

JUDGE C.R. MAGNEY STATE PARK

Grand Portage

CASCADE RIVER STATE PARK

Grand Marais

BUTTERWORT CLIFFS SCIENTIFIC NATURAL AREA

TEMPERANCE RIVER SP

Schroeder

GEORGE H. CROSBY– MANITOU SP

Finland

Manitou River

TETTEGOUCHE STATE PARK

Baptism River

1

53

61

SPLIT ROCK LIGHTHOUSE

Two Harbors

GOOSEBERRY RIVER STATE PARK

LAKE SUPERIOR

Saint Louis River

SKYLINE PKY

Carlton

210

Duluth

MICH

JAY COOKE STATE PARK

W Fk Bois Brule R

35

65

18

McGrath

BANNING STATE PARK

Sandstone

WISCONSIN

Danbury

Namekagon River

ST CROIX SP

23

ST. CROIX NAT WILD & SCENIC RIVER

Saint Croix R

Snake River

169

CHENGWATANA STATE FOREST

Valley

95

GOOSE CR NATURAL AREA

ST. CROIX WILD RIVER STATE PARK

8

10

Taylors Falls

35

INTERSTATE SP

Saint Croix Dalles

94

ST. CROIX NAT SCENIC RIVER

Saint Croix

Stillwater

94

ST PAUL

Precott

EASTERN MINNESOTA

25   0   25 Miles

25   0   25 Kilometers

ABOVE: *Among the animals inhabiting the Saint Croix woodlands are the bobcat (top), a nocturnal hunter that is well suited to winter, and numerous black bears (bottom), which are a game species in Minnesota.*

The Saint Croix is one of the cleanest, freest-running, and most ecologically intact large streams in the lower 48 states. Offering opportunities to camp, hunt, fish, canoe and boat, day-hike, and bird-watch, the river is one of the prime recreational streams in the upper Midwest. Bracketed by a mixed forest of pine and hardwoods, the Saint Croix is narrow and intimate in its upper reaches, descending peacefully through calm and gentle sections or crashing violently through rock-strewn, heart-stopping rapids.

Black bears, bobcat, and white-tailed deer roam the surrounding forests. Bald eagles and ospreys drift above, swooping in, talons ready, to pluck their dinner from the rushing waters. Smallmouth-bass fishing can be excellent, and many of the Saint Croix's numerous tributaries hold trout. Paralleling the stream for miles above Taylors Falls are seemingly endless, narrow side channels that twist and turn through thick bottomland forest where beavers, muskrat, herons, and many

ABOVE: *At Interstate State Park straddling the border of Wisconsin and Minnesota, a mirrorlike Saint Croix River slips quietly through the Dalles, high basalt cliffs that were deeply cut by a roaring glacial stream.*

species of waterfowl and songbirds abound. In the fall a quiet paddler can surprise flocks of brilliantly colored ducks that have assembled in secluded channels prior to migration. The marshes and quiet backwaters here seem far removed from human habitation.

Below Taylors Falls the river widens and slows. In its last 52-mile run to its confluence with the Mississippi, the Saint Croix is enclosed by an almost purely deciduous forest. Below Stillwater, the widening channel becomes better suited to large powerboats and yachts. Along these lower stretches, white bass, sauger, walleye, and crappies are particularly plentiful, although anglers may encounter more than 50 species of fish.

One of the loveliest places along the Saint Croix is **Interstate State Park❖,** a 293-acre site paralleling the river; an additional 1,400-acre park is across the river in Wisconsin. These two sister parks form the nation's first interstate park. The Minnesota unit is on Route 8 in the town of Taylors Falls. Its principal features are its glacial potholes and a high rock-

LEFT: *A native of Eurasia, the orange day lily has naturalized extensively in the region; here it blooms at Interstate State Park.*
RIGHT: *Red and white pine again grow atop slabs of basalt at Interstate State Park, where towering old-growth forests were extensively logged in the late 1800s.*

bound narrows known as the Saint Croix Dalles, where the river squeezes through a deep cut in the Precambrian basalt and plunges beneath sheer cliffs that rise to 150 feet on either side. Written into these rock faces is an eon of geologic history. The cliffs were formed nearly a billion years ago from a series of lava flows. For hundreds of thousands of years pulses of lava pushed up and out, depositing layer upon layer across the land, which accumulated to thicknesses of more than 20,000 feet. At the Dalles, ten of these layers can be seen in cross-section below 100 feet of sedimentary rock, once the bottom of a Paleozoic sea.

When glacial meltwater roared down this valley some 10,000 years ago, it cut through both the sedimentary and basaltic material (the more resistant basalt confined the torrent to a narrow gorge). The raging meltwater also left cliffside terraces pocked and pitted with potholes. Ground into the rock by swirling gravel-laden water, these holes range in size from small depressions to huge wells more than 10 feet across and 60 feet deep.

Twelve miles north of Interstate State Park on County Road 16, **Wild River State Park❖,** a 6,762-acre tract, abuts the southern end of **Chengwatana State Forest❖.** Encompassing a 17-mile corridor of protected woodland on the Minnesota side of the river, the park maintains an extensive trail system along most of its length. Small remnants of prairie and savanna dot the uplands. At the park's northern end, **Goose Creek Natural Area❖** is a particularly interesting natural site containing an unusual patchwork of habitats. Intermixed here are black ash forest, floodplain forest, lowland hardwood forest, and some tamarack swamp forest—an intimate and uncommon place. Also within the park is **Amador Prairie,** designated to protect and reestablish endangered prairie species such as big bluestem and blazing star prairie flowers. The area is divided into two sections of 110 acres and

ABOVE: *In Wild River State Park, a dramatic midday storm approaches Amador Prairie, where naturalists are gradually restoring native grasses and wildflowers by hand sowing seeds and setting periodic fires.*

65 acres, each with its own trailhead and interpretative sign. Coyotes and deer inhabit the prairie, as well as bullsnakes, the prey of hawks and other raptors wheeling overhead.

Of the many wooded streams that tumble to the Saint Croix from the western highlands, two rivers—some 15 miles north of the park—are of particular note: the Snake and the Kettle. Important log driving rivers during the cut-and-run clear-cutting of the Saint Croix Valley in the late 1800s, they were choked with silt and logging debris a hundred years ago, their waters flowing through a bare and ravaged land. In an admirable ecological turnabout, the rivers today are first-rate fishing and canoeing streams enclosed by dense second-growth woods and high cliffs.

The **Snake River**—the southernmost of the two—rises among alder, willow, and black spruce swamps in southern Aitkin County. Its remote upper reaches flow through thick mixed forests of paper birch, aspen, oak, maple, ash, elm, and balsam fir. Black spruce grows in the lowlands, and an occasional remnant white pine can be seen rising above the forest's canopy. About 10 miles below the town of McGrath, the river narrows and plunges through a set of granite gorges, making this area—as well as the lower 12 miles, which are almost continuous maps showing access points are available from the Minnesota Department of Natural Resources.) The river's name is English for a French translation of the Ojibwa *kanabec* or snake, a derisive term for their mortal enemies the Dakota, who lived around the headwaters and whom the Ojibwa later displaced.

Emptying into the Saint Croix a few miles upstream, the **Kettle River** is considered one of Minnesota's premier canoe streams and was the first to be included in the state's Wild and Scenic River System. The Kettle rises in several small tributaries flowing from an alder swamp and willow bog in west-central Carlton County. Like the Snake, most of the river is bounded by a thick mixed forest of fir, hardwoods, and scattered red and white pine remnants. The Kettle's most spectacular stretch is a deep sandstone gorge in the heart of **Banning State Park❖,** just off I-35 on Route 23 in Sandstone.

The Banning rapids are an extremely dangerous descent and a notorious challenge to kayakers, who must navigate a two-mile series of chutes, cascades, souse holes (backwater on the downstream sides of boulders), low rock overhangs, and boiling, boulder-strewn rapids. Plenty of other stretches here, however, are accessible to novice canoeists. Smallmouth bass, walleye, and northern pike are caught all along the river, as are sturgeon, redhorse, and channel catfish. The Kettle is also rich in wildlife, including black bears, otters, bobcat, beavers, mink and red and gray foxes.

The last seven miles of the Kettle River form the western boundary of the oldest Saint Croix riverside park. At more than 33,000 acres, **Saint Croix State Park❖,** on County Route 22, is also Minnesota's largest. Measuring more than 20 river miles from its northern end to its southern border, the park lies along an unspoiled wooded, island-dotted stretch of the Saint Croix. Several brooks, some containing trout, flow through the tract, twisting and turning through closed woods down to the river. The park offers a variety of camping facilities from primitive to RV and is a good put-in point for extended trips downstream.

LAKE SUPERIOR

About 45 miles northeast of Saint Croix State Park lies the city of Duluth, and beyond it the dramatic high scarps of Lake Superior and the wild highlands of the north. For visitors with no time to spare, I-35 is quick and direct; those interested in landscapes, however, find Route 23, the scenic road, the way to go. Leaving the Interstate at the Banning Park exit, Route 23 crosses old moraine and glacial lake bottom. Now heavily forested in aspen and paper birch and mostly devoid of people, this area once supported one of the finest stands of white pine in the region. Thousands of acres of towering giants stood here, trees reaching much more than 100 feet tall and up to 9 feet in circumference. In some places, the lowest branches of many of the tallest trees began some 50 feet above the forest floor, which was carpeted in duff (decayed organic debris) and pine needles and speckled here and there with sunlight that managed to penetrate the canopy. This dark, cavernous woods with little understory—which was cool in summer and sheltered from wind in winter—is virtually all gone now, scattered across the Midwest and beyond, converted to railroad ties, barn siding, and building timbers.

Many of the millennial events that shaped this region lie starkly exposed in **Jay Cooke State Park❖,** an 8,800-acre preserve spanning an imposing stretch of the lower Saint Louis River a few miles above its confluence with Lake Superior. A spectacular view of the park can be had from an overlook on the north side of Route 23, just before it descends into the river valley (the park entrance, however, is on Route 210 near Carlton). In the startling rock formations that enclose the river, a considerable slice of geologic history is visible. At its upstream end, the Saint Louis charges through a dramatic gorge of violently tilted graywacke and slate. The slate beds originated more than a billion years ago in the mud of an ancient seafloor. Buried and compacted, the mud became shale, which in turn was converted to slate by heat, pressure, and underground movement. In the process the buried slate and graywacke beds began to fold, fracture, and tilt on end, allowing molten rock to flow through the fractures and form black diabase dikes. Still visible today, the dikes were exposed some 12,000 to 10,000 years ago by meltwater pouring from a dying glacial lake, a giant precursor to Superior. Loaded with sediments and gravel, the glacial deluge cut Jay Cooke's spectacular gorge and bit deeply into the red clays of its former lake bottom. Deeply dissected banks of red clay still border the Saint Louis in the middle of the park and downstream.

A special place lies within this park. A small spring-fed stream plunges through **Hemlock Ravine Scientific and Natural Area**❖, home to an unusual stand of northern hardwoods, white pines, and a few eastern hemlocks. At the western edge of their range, the eastern hemlocks in this grove represent a quarter of all known hemlocks growing in Minnesota. The best time to visit the ravine is spring, when the hepatica, bloodroot, trillium, and Dutchman's-breeches are in bloom. (Group access to the steep slope requires a park permit.)

Duluth commands the westernmost end of the largest freshwater lake in the world. Occupying a natural trough of Precambrian rock, **Lake Superior**—more than 400 miles long, 160 miles wide, and up to 1,333 feet deep—is the overwhelmingly preeminent feature of this landscape. The largest of the Great Lakes dictates the flow of hundreds of rivers and more than a thousand regional streams. Creating its own local weather, Superior tempers both the heat of summer and cold of winter, and its storms are as awesome and legendary as any on the high seas.

One of several high vantage points above the lake is **Hawk Ridge**❖, on Skyline Parkway at the east end of Duluth. Not only is the ridge a fine place to observe Duluth harbor and the lake's western end, but the highland sits in the middle of a major migration corridor for hawks and a huge array of other birds. In the fall, migratory birds leave their summer homes in the Canadian north and begin their southward trek. When they reach Lake Superior, they funnel southwest to avoid flying over open water, taking advantage of the thermals coming off the high ridges above the shoreline, which the birds ride down on. They swing around the western end of the lake, winging directly over Duluth. Single-day raptor counts can be astonishing: 743 bald eagles, 23 golden eagles, 1,229 goshawks, 48,000 broad-winged hawks, 3,991 red-tailed hawks, 18 peregrines—although not all on the same single day! Numerous other species following the same route include snow geese, sandhill cranes, black-backed woodpeckers, Lapland longspurs, snow buntings, long-eared and northern saw-whet owls, and many types of songbirds. The bulk of the migration occurs from mid-September to late October. Because hawks traditionally ride ther-

OVERLEAF: *Tilted slabs of slate pierce the foaming current of the Saint Louis River in Jay Cooke State Park. Once Precambrian mud, these rocks contain the fossilized prints of ancient raindrops and ripples.*

Raptors of coniferous forests include the northern goshawk (left), which preys on snowshoe hares and grouse, and the powerful great horned owl (above) with its distinctive ear tufts.

mal currents, the best flight days tend to accompany cold fronts with winds from the northwest. On most days, hawks start flying a couple of hours after sunrise and peter out by mid-afternoon.

Hawk Ridge is part of a high basaltic lip that runs along Superior's northern shore from Duluth, past Grand Portage and the Pigeon River, and into Canada. A complicated mix of basalt, hard diabase, anorthosite, and rhyolite, this rock-lined shore has eroded in different ways at different locations. In some places the ridge slips subtly beneath Superior's frigid waters, in others it piles up as big-bouldered rubble, and elsewhere it plunges into the crashing surf in sheer 800-foot drops.

The basalts are the product of successive lava flows that nearly a billion years ago began pouring from cracks in the midcontinental crust, accumulating in places to depths of 23,000 feet. Eventually this bedrock sagged in the center, creating Superior's deep stone basin. Pounded by waves, scoured by moving ice, and split by thousands of centuries of hard freezes and sudden thaws, the rugged shoreline assumed its present form. In many places visitors would swear they were standing on the coast of Maine.

LAKE SUPERIOR'S NORTH SHORE

The Superior highlands rising behind the lake's northern shore were formed from rocky debris left by the last glacier, which climbed out of Superior's basin about 12,000 years ago. For centuries their southern reaches were covered with great stands of white pine intermixed with red pine and majestic northern hardwoods—sugar maples, basswood, yellow birches, and red oaks. In the north flourished a forest of aspen and birch. Conifer bogs and swamps, as well as groves of balsam fir and white spruce, occupied the low places. Today a century of industrial logging has cleared virtually all the pine and most of the big northern hardwoods. Although mainly aspen and birch grow here now—a proper standing crop for the region's pulp mills—bogs, swamps, and remnant stands of the old-growth forest still survive. Despite a heavy human hand, this land is still breathtaking. The **Superior Hiking Trail❖** offers an excellent way to experience these highlands. Winding over ridgelines, across rapids, along high cliffs, around inland lakes, and through remnant old-growth forests, the still-incomplete 200-mile footpath extends in long intermittent segments from Two Harbors to the Pigeon River area. Once finished, the trail will run unbroken for 280 miles from Duluth to Grand Portage, connecting eight state parks and several wayside rests.

A principal feature of the North Shore is the string of steep streams that surge off the south face of the highlands. The shoreline stretch between the Saint Louis River in the west and the Pigeon River in the east is riven by at least 28 such waterways. Rising in inland lakes, pools, swamps, bogs, and springs high in the hills, the streams come twisting, crashing, and churning down the flanks of the highlands, carving deep gorges in the basalt and often dropping from ledge to ledge in series of cascades. One of the more spectacular is the **Gooseberry River,** which makes its final astonishing plunge to Superior in three tiered falls and a series of small cascades that race through the heart of **Gooseberry**

Falls State Park❖, some 12 miles north of Two Harbors on Route 61. Of the thousands of stacked lava flows composing the North Shore, at least 30 can be found in the horizontally banded rock faces of the park. Some five miles east on Route 61 stands one of the most photographed historic structures in the nation. Built in 1909 to help ore ships maintain their bearings as they negotiated the dangerous rock-reefed waters leading into Duluth harbor, **Split Rock Lighthouse❖** stands atop a high scarp two miles upstream from the mouth of the **Split Rock River.** The lighthouse lamp—still floating in its original 250-pound bath of mercury—shone for 59 years before modern navigation systems made it obsolete. The land around the lighthouse is now a state park.

Some 15 miles up the coast from the lighthouse, the **Baptism River** (named for baptisms performed in it by seventeenth-century French missionaries) makes a particularly rugged descent into Lake Superior at **Tettegouche State Park❖.** The river and surrounding park are noted for impressive waterfalls and diverse shoreline landscape. In its last ten miles, the Baptism descends more than 700 feet in a series of cascades, foaming rapids, and falls, with drops of 70 feet. The variety of rocks— diabase intrusions, rhyolite, breccia rubble—make the shoreline at Tettegouche particularly rugged and decidedly scenic. At Palisade Head and Shovel Point, two prominent headlands, the pounding Superior surf has carved rock arches and water-level caves into the cliffs' basaltic lower reaches, leaving the harder rhyolite above intact. In the highlands—above the white cedar and black ash wetlands, above the aspen-birch groves—vestiges of the former forest survive, fine remnant stands of old-growth northern hardwoods. A section of the **Superior Hiking Trail❖** that winds through such an area can be reached from the highway by a footpath paralleling the river.

A little more than ten miles northeast of Tettegouche on Route 61, the lower reaches of the Manitou River cut through the heart of **George H. Crosby–Manitou State Park❖** (take Route 1 north to Finland, and County Route 7 east for eight miles). In its final seven miles, the river plunges over eight waterfalls and a series of continuous rapids. Within

RIGHT: *On a rocky promontory overlooking a wintry Lake Superior, the 1909 Split Rock Lighthouse stands unblinking. Modern technology has snuffed the light that once warned of treacherous shoals above Duluth.*

LEFT: *In a narrow, treelined gorge, Cascade Falls charges over a series of rocky terraces in its tumultuous descent to Lake Superior.*
ABOVE RIGHT: *The nodding flowers of the harebell, a member of the bluebell family, dot summer meadows along Superior's North Shore.*
BELOW RIGHT: *A subtle still life of gray-green lichens and golden "honey cap" mushrooms festoons a tree trunk in Cascade River State Park.*

the park are patches of old-growth northern hardwoods, including a fine stand of ancient yellow birch and white cedar. Named for the mining magnate and banker who donated the property to the state, Crosby-Manitou is the most primitive property in the state park system. Camping here is strictly tenting—most of the 21 tent sites are scattered along the Manitou's churning rapids and falls—and reaching the sites requires a bracing hike and energetic climb through thick forest. The park is the western trailhead of another section of the Superior Hiking Trail; the portion east to the Caribou State Wayside is particularly interesting because its midsection crosses an impressive geologic fault.

Continue east on Route 61 through the town of Schroeder to the Cross and Temperance rivers. A looping drive into the highlands—on Forest Road (FR) 343 to FR 166 east to the Sawbill Trail and then back to 61—is well worth the time. Much of FR 343 runs through a forest of ancient white cedar, a stand that somehow escaped the logging and subsequent fires that devastated these highlands. Unlike the terrain to the southwest, the uplands here are peppered with lakes, ponds, and marshes, which stabilize the flow of the Superior-bound rivers that drain them.

ABOVE: *Looking a bit like a misshapen crone, a weathered white cedar called the Witch Tree stands sentinel on Superior's Hat Point. The 400-year-old specimen is part of the Grand Portage Indian Reservation.*

The gorge of the lower Temperance River, which cuts through **Temperance River State Park❖,** is deep and so narrow that some of the falls are not even visible from the river's edge. Potholes in rock ledges adjacent to the river, routed out by turbulent gravel-loaded water, probably inspired the river's Ojibwa name, *Kawimbash,* or Deep Hollow River. It received its current name in the mid-1800s, when some droll soul noted that the Temperance, unlike other rivers along the North Shore, had no gravel bar at its mouth.

Perhaps nowhere else on the North Shore has the erosive artistry of rushing water been so creative as in the plunging gorge of the **Cascade River.** Located about 20 miles up the coast from the Temperance, the Cascade is the centerpiece of **Cascade River State Park❖,** which runs along the coast for several miles. The river is named for its spectacular drop over a series of prominent ledges in its last three-mile descent to Lake Superior. Falling some 900 feet over that distance— 120 feet in the final quarter mile—this river is an awesome sight, particularly in the late spring. Equally exquisite in its own way is a little-known state scientific and natural area that hugs the shoreline east of the river. **Butterwort Cliffs Scientific and Natural Area❖,** a 50-acre strip of wet basalt ledge, harbors an uncommon assemblage of rare

Above: *As lava cooled, the basalt cliffs at Artist Point near Grand Marais split into pillarlike formations; the sections at top and bottom hardened first, causing vertical fractures that created the columns.*

arctic-alpine plants that include northern eyebright, a short lavender-flowered plant once used for eye disorders, and the namesake butterwort, a carnivorous species that captures insects with its sticky leaves. A pleasing remoteness suffuses this place where delicate flowers and grasses grow among the multicolored lichen-covered rocks. (A permit from park headquarters is needed to visit this SNA, which is closed from May 1 to August 15 to protect a nesting colony of herring gulls.)

Of the North Shore's myriad streams, the most historically significant is the **Pigeon River,** which forms part of the Canadian border. Rising in South Lake, hard against a low divide that separates the watersheds of Hudson Bay and Lake Superior, the Pigeon makes a dramatic 60-mile run to the big lake. Its last 20 miles are a continuous series of cascades, violent rapids, and waterfalls, including **Pigeon Falls,** a breathtaking drop of nearly 100 feet near the river's mouth. For almost 200 years, from the mid-1600s to the 1840s, the river was a major access route to the fur riches of the North American interior.

Grand Portage Bay, a sheltered cove some five miles west of the Pigeon's mouth, was the eastern terminus for a network of lakes, rivers, and footpaths that extended west all the way to the Athabasca River in Alberta. In its heyday, this route was called the Voyageur Highway after

the colorful French-Canadian cargo haulers, explorers, and traders on whose backs and birch-bark canoes the fur trade was built. Today the **Grand Portage** is the 8.5-mile canoe carry that bypasses the last 20 miles of the lower Pigeon, which cannot be navigated. Climbing northwest from the bay, the portage wends its way up a low pass in the highlands to Fort Charlotte, situated about one mile upriver from a particularly spectacular stretch of the Pigeon known as the Cascades. For many of today's canoeists, crossing the portage is still a rite of passage.

At the eastern end of the portage is **Grand Portage National Monument❖,** which features a replica of a 1790s fur-trading depot. Here 12-man Montreal canoes, which hauled up to three tons of cargo and weathered repeated lake crossings, arrived from the Saint Lawrence to exchange supplies for furs from the interior. Annually, tons of pelts—the fruits of an ongoing slaughter of otters, mink, marten, wolves, lynx, and of course beaver—departed from here for Montreal and the capitals of Europe. The post was abandoned in 1805, when the U.S. government announced that it would levy taxes on all goods passing over the portage. Based principally on beaver, the fur industry died here after fashions changed in the 1840s.

By car, the closest access to the sensational falls and rapids of the lower Pigeon River is from **Grand Portage State Park❖** in the town of Grand Portage. A half-mile foot trail at the park leads to High Falls, the largest falls on the river.

ABOVE: *The northern flicker roams throughout Minnesota's woods. A member of the woodpecker family, the berry-loving bird is chiefly a ground-feeder; ants form the bulk of its diet.*

LEFT: *A winter favorite of the avian population because of its tasty scarlet berries, an American mountain ash catches the morning sun near Grand Marais.*

OVERLEAF: *Dawn brings its vivid palette to a classic North Shore landscape as the Susie Islands float between flaming sky and rosy waters near Grand Portage.*

THE NORTHERN TIER:
WILDERNESS, WOLVES, AND THE IRON RANGE

R ich in human and natural history, much of Minnesota's remote northern borderlands are as wild and roadless as they
were when French adventurer Jacques de Noyons first saw
them in 1688. All along the Canadian border—from Rainy
Lake and Voyageurs National Park east through the boundary waters
to Lake Superior and the tip of Minnesota at Pigeon River—lies an untamed, watery wilderness. In this spectacular rockbound region, dense
forests blanket a land peppered with hundreds of blue lakes.

This area stands on exposed granite, a southern extension of the Precambrian bedrock core of North America known as the Canadian
Shield. The lakes strewn across the rugged rock faces here contain
water that has pooled along ice-troweled weaknesses, fissures, and
other anomalies on the shield's granite face. West of the Vermilion
River, the bedrock gradually disappears, and the land levels out. Beyond the Little Fork River stretches a boggy lake plain, the floor of the
eastern arm of Glacial Lake Agassiz, which once occupied the state's
northern tier as far west as North Dakota. Peatland covers much of this
vast basin—a remote expanse of sphagnum moss and tamarack, of
spruce, white cedar, and black-ash bogs that from above dissolve into a
surreal mosaic patterned in countless shades of green.

South of these border lands, north-central Minnesota is a region of

LEFT: *Basswood Falls sits on the Canada border at the edge of Minnesota's Boundary Waters Canoe Area Wilderness, a million acres of
isolated lakes, churning rapids, fertile marshes, and endless forest.*

ABOVE: *Denis Gale's 1860 watercolor* The Portage *documents the Voyageur Highway, the fur traders' water and overland route to the interior.*

ecological and topographical chaos, a kaleidoscope of moraines, bedrock highlands, and flat former lake plains that express themselves in thickly forested hills, lowland bogs and cedar swamps, sandy plains, and an abundance of lakes. The rich mix of ecosystems in this area, a legacy of the last glacial age, supported a wealth of wildlife and game. The ancestral home of the Dakota, the region was lost to the invading Ojibwa in the early 1700s. The Ojibwa in turn fell victim to the Europeans, who saw in north-central Minnesota a treasure trove of natural resources, which they subsequently mined to exhaustion—first its fur-bearing wildlife, then its pine, and finally its iron ore. Today the region's major sources of income are tourism and timber, mainly aspen for pulp.

This chapter's itinerary begins in Ely, a major gateway to the northern wilderness of the boundary waters, and then travels west along the Canadian border to Voyageurs National Park. The driving route heads south to the Iron Range, southwest to Grand Rapids, and then northwest into the morainic highlands and Chippewa National Forest. Turning west on Route 1, it proceeds along the southern edge of the Red Lake basin to Route 72, where it heads north to culminate in the patterned peatlands.

OVERLEAF: *In Superior National Forest, a winter sun brightens an aspen grove lying under a thick blanket of snow along the Gunflint Trail.*

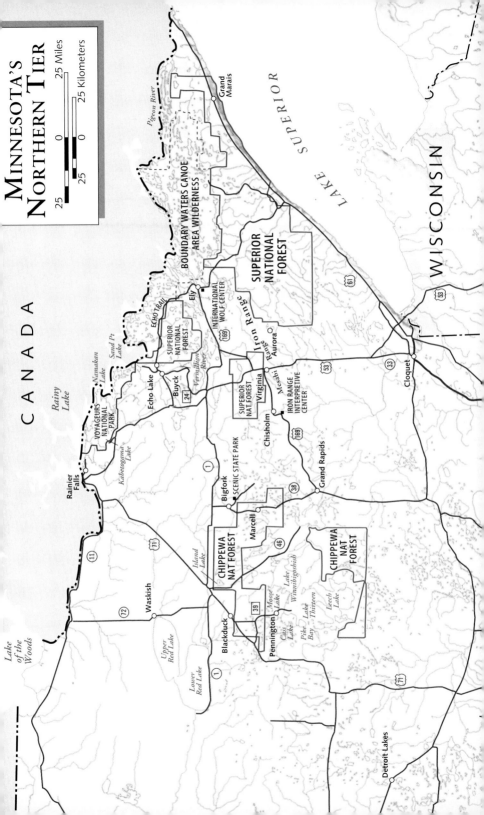

MINNESOTA'S NORTHERN TIER

25 Miles

25 Kilometers

0

0

25

25

CANADA

Lake of the Woods

Rainy Lake

Namakan Lake

Sand Pt. Lake

Pigeon River

LAKE SUPERIOR

WISCONSIN

Rainier Falls

VOYAGEURS NATIONAL PARK

Kabetogama Lake

BOUNDARY WATERS CANOE AREA WILDERNESS

Grand Marais

SUPERIOR NATIONAL FOREST

ECHO TRAIL

Echo Lake

Buyck

24

SUPERIOR NATIONAL FOREST

Vermillion River

Ely

INTERNATIONAL WOLF CENTER

169

Iron Range

Range

Aurora

61

Virginia

Mesabi

Chisholm

IRON RANGE INTERPRETIVE CENTER

169

53

33

Cloquet

53

SUPERIOR NAT FOREST

SCENIC STATE PARK

Bigfork

1

Grand Rapids

38

Marcell

Island Lake

CHIPPEWA NAT FOREST

46

CHIPPEWA NAT FOREST

11

Waskish

12

Upper Red Lake

Lower Red Lake

1

Blackduck

39

Pennington

Moose Lake

Cass Lake

Lake Winnibigoshish

Pike Bay

Lake Thirteen

Leech Lake

71

Detroit Lakes

BOUNDARY WATERS AND VOYAGEURS NATIONAL PARK

Stretching along two-thirds of Minnesota's northern edge, from the mouth of the Pigeon River on Lake Superior to the shores of Lake of the Woods, the border lakes region of the state is a land of rivers, lakes, and forests. Three million acres lie within the **Superior National Forest❖,** which maintains the woodlands for pulp and paper production and manages the land and water for recreational uses. Fifty major hiking trails crisscross the forest, which also contains dozens of campgrounds and about 200 primitive campsites. Strewn throughout this country are more than 2,000 lakes connected by an extensive network of portages, rivers, and streams. Many primitive roads accommodate off-road vehicles, and snowmobile trails are found throughout much of the forest.

ABOVE: **With its haunting call, the common loon, the official state bird, personifies Minnesota's unspoiled boundary waters. The loon nests only in pristine areas.**

RIGHT: **A painterly view of Boundary Waters' Lake Agnes combines lily pads, a submerged rock, and reflections of the clouds above.**

The heart of Superior National Forest is the unparalleled **Boundary Waters Canoe Area Wilderness (BWCAW)❖.** Encompassing more than a million acres and extending nearly 150 miles along the Canadian border, the BWCAW contains 1,500 miles of water routes and some 1,000 lakes of 10 acres or more, most connected by a network of footpaths. It abuts the southern edge of Ontario's huge Quetico Provincial Park, a similarly run wilderness area in Canada; together the two cover more than two million acres. This vast roadless landscape shelters isolated rockbound lakes, meandering sedge-meadow rivers, black spruce and tamarack bogs, quiet beaver ponds, thundering falls and cascading rapids, granite scarps, and astonishing, seemingly endless forests—woodlands of spruce, black ash, and balsam fir, of northern white cedar and old-growth red and white pine, of jack pine, aspen, and birch. In this land, as wild as any in the lower 48 states, the echoing howls of wolves and eerie calls of loons are as

ABOVE: *An eastern timber wolf lopes out of the woods at the International Wolf Center in Ely. Now integrated into Minnesota's northern ecosystem, more wolves live here than in any other state except Alaska.*

much a part of the landscape as the lakes and trees. Wildlife abounds: black bears, moose, lynx, and white-tailed deer roam the forests; otters, mink, muskrat, and beavers ply the streams and lakes; and eagles, ospreys, and hawks work the ridges and shorelines. Vast stretches of unbroken forest harbor owls and myriad species of songbirds. Waterfowl—scaup, teal, mallard, canvasbacks, and others—inhabit these wilderness lakes.

Travel in this wild, watery landscape is strictly by canoe or on foot. Indeed, the wildness of the area has been preserved by restricting motorboats to a handful of lakes and by strictly controlling the number of people in the park at one time. From May through September, entry is by permit, and reservations are recommended at least four months in advance; camping is at designated sites only, on a first-come-first-served basis. Because there are no concessions in the park, visitors must bring their food and shelter on their backs or in their canoes (outfitters are located in Grand Marais in the east and Ely in the central region). Hunting and trapping are allowed within the BWCAW, and the fishing is excellent, particularly for walleye, northern pike, bass, muskellunge, crappies, perch, and trout.

Visitors who arrive at the right time of year—early summer or fall—and are willing to paddle and portage can reach areas where they see no one for days and experience the wilderness as it once was, although most of the virgin pine has been cut and the land covered with regrowth. Indeed, the lakes and portages traveled by canoeists today are probably the same routes used by the Dakota and later the Ojibwa, and the footpaths are likely those plied by European voyageurs during the heyday of the fur trade. Although most of the virgin white pine was logged long ago, little else has changed since the French explorer Sieur de la Vérendrye passed through in 1731 seeking the "western sea."

Like most of the rest of the state, the BWCAW's rock-rimmed lakes and forested granite ridges bear the stamp of moving ice. Here the creative force was the weight of the glacier as it ground on weaker surfaces in the granite highland. The lakes strung along the border to the northeast, for instance, swarm along an east-west axis. Gouged by gravel-studded southbound ice, they lie in parallel troughs of slate, softer rock than the granite ridges separating them; before the ice arrived, they were river valleys carved by preglacial streams. To the southwest, around long, lean Knife and Moose lakes, bodies of water have formed in zigzag patterns along old fault lines where weakened rock lay exposed to the full force of the moving ice. Ice also sculpted the region's more uniform rock, leaving countless other bodies of water and an incomparably beautiful land.

A major feature of these northern landscapes is the timber wolf. In fact, most of the wolves in the lower 48 live in this area of Minnesota. An estimated 2,000 members of this federally threatened species live here, most of them along the northern tier. Once demonized throughout the western world—and still despised by many—the wolf has recently made a comeback. The population is now expanding thanks to

---

OVERLEAF: *A solitary paddler glides out to enjoy a spectacular technicolor sunset on Lake Kabetogama in Voyageurs National Park. Kabetogama is actually a deep bay at the south end of huge Rainy Lake.*

several decades of protection and a glut of white-tailed deer, its principal prey. Deer dramatically increased after the big pine forests were cut and replaced by aspens, which the deer prefer to eat. A recommended stop in Ely is the **International Wolf Center❖,** on Route 169 at the east end of town. Dedicated to educating visitors about this much-maligned predator, the center features a resident wolf pack, multimedia presentations, and the award-winning Wolves and Humans exhibit. The presentations and exhibits explore wolf biology and behavior, as well as the myths that have surrounded the animal through history, the problems it now faces, and the intense controversy it continues to generate.

Those not inclined to venture into the BWCAW can experience this stark and lovely land by traveling the **Echo Trail** (County Route 116), a road that runs north from Ely and west to Echo Lake and County Route 24. Skirting the southern edge of the main body of the BWCAW, this highly scenic route traverses a variety of habitats and much hilly and forested terrain.

County Route 24 leads south to the town of Buyck and the **Vermilion River.** Situated near the river's midsection, the town is a good jumping-off place for canoe trips downstream (upstream accesses are off CR 24 to the south.) Rising in big, sprawling Vermilion Lake, some dozen miles south, the Vermilion River winds its way north through wild-rice beds and dense forests of spruce-fir, pine, and aspen-birch. Much of the Vermilion's 40-mile course is wild and fairly remote; except for difficult rapids around its headwaters and at its lower end, easy paddling makes it a good canoe river. About a mile above its mouth, the river surges between sheer 60-foot walls of granite before emptying into Crane Lake. In the late 1600s, the river became an important trade route for French fur traders who ranged across the border lakes region. In the latter 1800s and early decades of this century, it was an important log-driving river.

Crane Lake, at the west end of the BWCAW, is one of several access points to 200,000 more acres of protected water and forest to the northwest in **Voyageurs National Park❖.** Occupying the southern end of Rainy Lake, Minnesota's only national park encompasses 30

RIGHT: *Intensely scenic, watery Voyageurs National Park encloses many lakes and hundreds of wooded islands. Here a secluded marsh stretches along the shoreline of Moose Bay, one of Lake Kabetogama's many inlets.*

ABOVE: *A moose and her two calves casually browse among the lush aquatic vegetation along the Nina Moose River.*
RIGHT: *Soaring white pines shelter a secluded campsite, accessible only by water, at La Bontys Point on Lake Kabetogama.*

lakes and some 1,600 islands, which shelter wolves, nesting bald eagles, and loons. Largely a water preserve, Voyageurs is dominated by four huge lakes—Rainy, Kabetogama, Namakan, and Sand Point—that frame the enormous Kabetogama Peninsula, fringed with a multitude of bays, marshes, and smaller islands. With some substantial exceptions, Voyageurs is nearly as primitive as the BWCAW. Watercraft that are allowed within the park include—besides canoes—motorboats, houseboats, and sailboats. Snowmobiles are permitted on designated trails in the winter as well. Entry permits are not required, and there are no limits on group sizes or number of people in the park.

The preserve lies along the old Voyageur Highway, the ancient system of lakes, streams, and footpaths established by Native Americans. This area was first described by French explorer Sieur de la Vérendrye, who traveled over Rainy Lake in 1731. Soon after, the highway became the route of choice for French-Canadian trappers and traders who moved furs over it from the northern forests to Montreal and thence to Europe. Commandeered by the British after their 1759 victory at Quebec during the French and Indian War, the route eventually extended as far west as Fort Chipewyan on Lake Athabasca in Alberta, a 3,000-mile trade network dominated by the powerful North West Company.

At the outlet of Rainy Lake, now on the park's western edge, stood

Athabasca House, a trading center and rendezvous where the Athabasca brigades sold the furs they had collected during the winter and resupplied themselves with goods arriving from the east over the Grand Portage. The post at Rainy allowed the men to get back to the far northwest before the weather closed in. Today the park maintains visitor centers at Rainy Lake (east of International Falls off Route 11) and Kabetogama Lake (off Route 53 on County Route 122) where naturalist-led cruises depart to tour the park.

THE IRON RANGE AND CHIPPEWA NATIONAL FOREST

Perhaps nowhere else on the Northern Tier have the land and its residents been more affected by its natural resources than in the hardscrabble country south of Vermilion. Two billion to one billion years ago, chance provided this region with significant quantities of elemental iron in the molten soup that became the continent's foundation rock. For millennia the iron was present in its reduced form in marine basins in silica-laden waters. When these waters welled up into oxygen-rich shallows, the iron and silica precipitated and settled in thin layers on the bottom. Through subsequent millennia, this iron oxide was concentrated and incorporated into the sediments in three narrow iron-bearing bands—some of the richest on the planet—running roughly parallel to

ABOVE: *A bald eagle surveys his domain. Nearly wiped out by DDT, eagles are now recovering; Minnesota harbors one of the largest breeding populations in the lower 48.*

one another across Minnesota's northeast region.

The largest band—and the heart of Minnesota's Iron Range—is the **Mesabi Range,** where a large vein runs along the southern flank of the low granite hills of Giants Range, an exposed bedrock section of the ancient transcontinental Laurentian Divide. Some 120 miles long and 1 to 3 miles wide, the Mesabi runs southwest from the town of Aurora to Grand Rapids. Lying close to the surface, the ore was easily accessible, and open-pit mining began in 1890.

By the 1950s ore from this range alone constituted about a third of the world's total iron ore production, and prosperity quickly followed. When extraction of the richest ore, hematite, peaked in 1955, the industry switched to taconite, a lower grade ore requiring more costly processing. Since the early 1980s, however, the fabrication of high-tech substitutes for steel and new mines and international processing facilities have caused the industry to decline.

As the vein nears depletion after nearly a century, mining's dramatic effect on the land is abundantly evident. Visitors can sense the devastation by driving down the spine of the Mesabi Range, west from the town of Virginia on Route 169. Where pine and fir and hills of aspen-birch once stood, a moonscape of tiered open pits now snakes through treeless hills of waste rock. Even the lands that have been restored seem oddly shaped and look a little too perfect. Fish-stocked lakes, clear and eerily blue under rust-colored banks, occupy some of the old pits. The complete story of the Iron Range is told through artifacts, graphics, and videos at the **Ironworld Discovery Center❖,** just south of Route 169 west of Chisholm. It's well worth a visit.

The vast north-central region of Minnesota west of the Iron Range—from Route 1 in the north to Saint Cloud in the south, and from Cloquet in the east to Detroit Lakes in the west—is a terrifically complicated mix of landforms and forest ecosystems. The terrain ranges from steeply rolling hills to level plains. Most of the land is heavily wooded, laced with rivers, and strewn with lakes, some—such as Cass, Winnibigoshish, Leech, and Mille Lacs—of considerable size. Forests are a rich mix of conifer swamps and bogs, groves of aspen-birch, and stands of spruce and fir. This complicated landscape is the result of the last glaciation—a series of advances and retreats of ice fronts from the west, north, and east that came and went across the region over the course of some 100,000 years. Glacial debris from different lobes, deposited at different times, lies jumbled together.

Across the heart of this kaleidoscope of landscapes lies 1.6-million-acre **Chippewa National Forest❖.** Encompassing essentially all the land between Deer River in the east and Cass Lake in the west, and extending north from south of Leech Lake almost to Route 1, the "Chip" contains nearly the full range of the state's northern forest ecosystems. The national forest administers only 600,000 acres of this landscape; the rest is managed by various counties, the state, the Leech Lake Indian tribe, and private landowners. Within the Chip's ice-worked topography are some 700 lakes, 920 miles of streams, more than 150,000 acres of wetlands, one of the largest breeding populations of bald eagles in the lower 48 states, and a few impressive stands of remnant old-growth red and white pine forest. More than 160 miles of trails lead to a number of special places within the forest, including Native American and state historical sites, wildlife areas, old-growth stands, and a variety of habitats.

The forest visitor centers in Cass Lake, Deer River, Marcell, Walker, and Blackduck can provide information about specific sites within the national forest. Among the special habitats along the Chippewa's northeast and eastern perimeter is an island in **Island Lake,** south of Route 1 and east of Route 46, that shelters a fine grove of white cedar, a community once fairly common across northern Minnesota but now in decline; and the **Lost Forty,** a stand of old-growth red and white pine on the shores of Coddington Lake that miraculously escaped clear-cutting because of a mapping error.

A series of bogs and wetlands stretch along County Route 39 south of Blackduck. **Webster Lake,** a wetland at the west end of Rabideau Lake, contains an unusual abundance of carnivorous linear sundew plants; **Gilfillan Lake,** west of Route 39 and north of County Route 22,

harbors an abundance of orchids and a white spruce forest; **Pennington Bog,** west of Pennington, a state scientific and natural area that requires a permit from the Minnesota Department of Natural Resources to visit, is another wetland supporting a profusion of beautiful and unusual plant species. The **Ten Section Area,** at the south end of Cass Lake, features a large stand of red and white pine. Saved by conservationists early in the century, the Ten Section site was set aside at the height of clear-cutting. That fight, one of the nation's early conservation versus industry confrontations, led eventually to the formation of the Chippewa National Forest, the first national forest east of the Mississippi.

Visitors can also experience the geology of this area directly by heading north from Grand Rapids on Route 38. After about 15 miles of thickly forested hills, the highway begins to twist, buck, and turn as it ascends a steeply rolling landscape of forested hills and small, marsh-lined kettle lakes. These are the Suomi Hills, actually an end moraine of a glacier once centered above North Dakota. Five or six miles north of Marcell, the road passes a field of braided eskers. This series of parallel ridges visible to the east are actually sediments of streams that once flowed through ice tunnels at the bottom of the glacier.

At the town of Bigfork, take County Route 7 east seven miles to

Left: *Once the floor of a winding subglacial river, this hilly esker in Scenic State Park is now home to a fine stand of old-growth red pines.*
Right: *Mushrooms found growing in Voyageurs National Park include the scarlet fairy helmet (top) and the strange purple club coral (bottom).*

Scenic State Park❖. Within this 2,000-acre tract are a number of glacial landforms typical of this north-central region, including a well-delineated esker—a long, narrow, steep forested ridge that nearly bisects the two lakes flanking it. The ridge is the sand and gravel bed of a river that once flowed beneath the ice; the lakes on either side are the water-filled depressions left by buried ice that melted under the overlying glacial debris. (The same process created the braided eskers to the south along Route 38.) Other glacial features in this park include the deep, steep-sided kettle lakes, also formed from buried ice, as well as several kames. Of particular note in this pretty park are the stands of old-growth red and white pine forests that stand at either end of the trough lakes and cover the esker. Reminders of the vast pinery that once blanketed much of this region, many of these huge trees are more than 100 years old.

THE NORTHWEST: PEATLANDS AND WILDERNESS

Northwest of the park and due north of Chippewa National Forest is a vast land of incomparable wildness—arguably the only true wilderness left in the state. Extending over 450 square miles, the **Red Lake Peatlands❖** constitute the largest continuous bog in the lower 48 states. They occupy the floor of Glacial Lake Agassiz, a gigantic pool of meltwater caught between melting ice to the north and moraines far to the south. In Minnesota, Upper and Lower Red Lake, Lake of the Woods to the north, and a few small lakes are all that remains of the vast lake.

In this gently sloping, desolate, and painfully beautiful country, there are no human structures—no trails, no roads, no portage markers, no campsites. The only signs of human activity are a few overgrown winter logging roads and remnant ditch lines left from an ill-fated 1909–17 attempt to drain a portion of the flat, waterlogged lands for agriculture and

129

logging. This land of sphagnum moss, spruce and tamarack bogs, sedge fens, and swamps dominated by white cedar and black ash is home to timber wolves and moose, which range across the region. In the 1920s caribou could be found here, before hunting, logging, and settlement extirpated them from the state. In the spring, leatherleaf, its bell-shaped white flowers drooping like Christmas ornaments, grows across the treeless bog. Labrador tea carpets the forested areas. Meadowlike sedges dominate the fens, and between islands of tamarack, dwarf birch and black spruce roll on a hummocky sea of sphagnum moss.

A cold, wet climate and high water table have reduced vegetative decomposition to a near standstill here. Low temperatures severely limit the numbers of decomposers—worms, fungi, bacteria, and slime molds—that process dead plant matter. Instead of disintegrating, dead plant material simply accumulates in compacted layers. The resulting environment, low in oxygen and highly acidic, further reduces decomposers. For thousands of years, these peatlands have deepened and expanded over the lake bottom, supporting rare plants and animals.

From above, the sedge meadows, spruce and tamarack islands, and sphagnum hummocks dissolve into a huge surreal surface—a many-hued green palette of swirls, parallel lines, elliptical blobs, trails of tears, and winding ribbons of water. This rare landscape of patterned peatland exists in only a few other places in the world (Siberia, Sweden, Alaska). Composed of ovoid and teardrop-shaped islands, raised bogs and water-tracks, pools, ridges, and narrow natural drainage channels, the mosaic patterns are strikingly enhanced by the different plant communities that blanket them. Although these intricate designs are formed mainly by moving water, precisely how the system produces these effects remains a mystery. Unfortunately, these lands are generally inaccessible to casual travelers, except those willing to get wet or camp in winter, when the bog freezes. One of the few places to experience them is Route 72 about 12 miles north of Waskish. Water-filled ditches flank the road, but a wooden bridge east of Route 72 allows visitors to walk into the bog, where high rubber boots and a compass are musts for any hike through these fens, spruce islands, and hummocks of quaking sphagnum.

RIGHT: *A meandering river winds through the flat peatlands of Pine Island State Forest in isolated northwestern Minnesota. Water flows constantly through this vast expanse of sphagnum moss and stunted trees.*

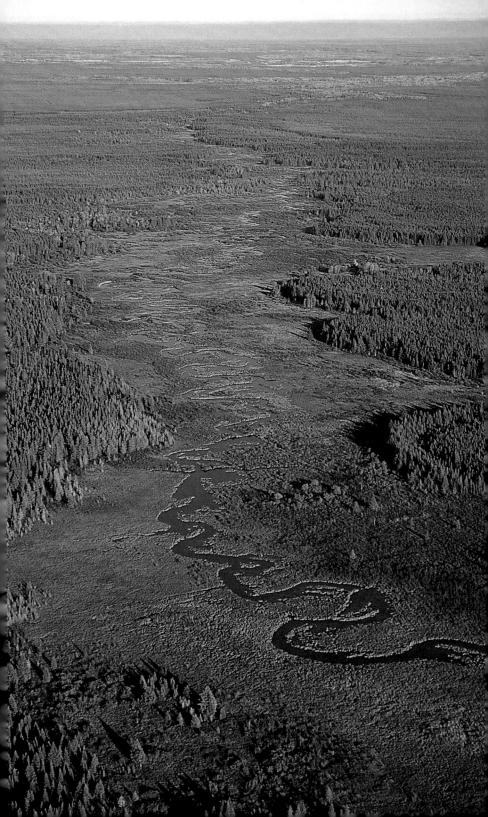

NORTH DAKOTA

PART TWO

N O R T H   D A K O T A

The two best things about North Dakota, claims a familiar joke, are the east and west ends of Interstate 94, the state's nearly perfectly straight east-west border-to-border highway. In fact, the implication that nothing lies between them is anything but true.

Although North Dakota indeed contains much flat, treeless land, in other areas clear rivers run under high wooded escarpments, and among aspen-forested hills, quiet lakes echo with the calls of loons. Steep, undulating prairies, flecked with ponds, potholes, and marshes, are crowded with ducks, geese, and shorebirds. One of America's legendary rivers, the Missouri, winds through the state, and miles of wild, windswept land—dotted with buttes, coulees, and canyons and washed in every color of the rainbow—sweep grandly to distant horizons.

Nearly everywhere in the state, the creative hand was ice. Grinding down from Canada, probably about 25,000 years ago, the last glacier crunched its way across North Dakota, coming to rest where the eastern bank of the Missouri River lies today. In the process it blocked the natural flow of many rivers—the Cannonball, Heart, Knife, Yellowstone, and Little Missouri—forcing their waters east and south. When the ice finally melted, the rivers had cut a deep permanent trench, where their combined courses are now known as the Missouri River. Buried for much of its length under the vast impounded waters of Lake Sakakawea, the great river today retains few areas where it flows as it did when Lewis and Clark charted its course almost two centuries ago.

When the last ice melted here some 12,000 years ago, it left behind a collection of distinctly different physiographic regions arranged roughly east-west across the state. Straddling the eastern border with Minnesota is the dead-level lake plain of Glacial Lake Agassiz, a huge body of water that was trapped between the ice sheet to the north and a moraine more than a hundred miles to the south.

PRECEDING PAGES: *On the rolling plains of central North Dakota near Mc-Clusky, a prairie pothole glistens under the midday sun. These countless small wetlands once supported sky-darkening flocks of waterfowl.*

West of the ancient lake, the land gradually rises into a vast till plain, gently undulating terrain covered by thick glacial debris. Just a century ago this biologically rich plain was blanketed by a vast sea of grasses—a magnificent prairie laced with wetlands, freshwater marshes, saline ponds, and small lakes that supported huge herds of bison, pronghorn, elk, and wolves, as well as millions of waterfowl. Today, an immense green checkered carpet of sugar beets, potatoes, corn, and soybeans grows across the lake plain, while spring wheat, durum, barley, flax, oats, and rye have replaced the prairie and much of the wetlands to the west.

West of the till plain, the land rises to a wetlands-peppered highland known as the Missouri Coteau. This high, steeply rolling pothole-riddled rangeland is the largest of three similarly fashioned highlands rising above the till plain. Smaller and isolated, the other two are the thickly wooded Turtle Mountains that lie to the north along the Canada–North Dakota border and the rumpled Prairie Coteau, which stands in the very southeastern corner of the state. The coteaus were created when ancient ice sheets deposited across existing highlands unconsolidated rocky sediment, which insulated pockets of ice below. When the climate warmed and the ice finally melted, the glacial debris above collapsed, forming a hilly, lake-strewn region. Running along the eastern side of the Missouri River from the South Dakota border to Canada, the Missouri Coteau is the heart of the state's share of the North American Prairie Pothole Region—the so-called duck factory of the nation because it produces annually about half of the waterfowl in the lower 48 states.

The west flank of the Missouri Coteau is a rolling, hilly plain that descends to the Missouri River—a winding strip of grassland that geographers consider the eastern edge of the Great Plains, that stretch of broad, mostly flat land that gradually swells to meet the Rockies. West of the Missouri is country fabricated from the soft clay, sand, mud, and silt that washed off the eastern flanks of the rising Rocky Mountains some 55 million years ago. In this dry country of softly rolling hills, mid-grass and short-grass prairie are laced with myriad woody draws. Remnants of a vanished landscape, solitary buttes capped by hard sandstone or lignite-baked rock punctuate the grassy vistas. This classic western landscape finds its most spectacular expression in the far southwestern reaches of the state, in the wild, colorful, and fantastically eroded badlands of the Little Missouri River.

From lake bed to prairie, highlands to badlands, North Dakota's landscapes are fascinating and complex—and richly rewarding for those who seek them out.

EAST OF THE MISSOURI:
GREAT DRIFT PLAIN
AND HIGH COTEAUS

An endless plain," "an empty silence," "level as a floor," "a dull uniformity of prospect, spread out immense," "a vast ocean," and "breakers of bluejoint" are descriptions of North America's great northeastern prairies in which writers strike similar themes. Delivered and sculpted by moving and melting ice, much of North Dakota's share of the extensive ecosystem—especially east and north of the Missouri River—presents a limitless undulating landscape that inspires comparisons to swelling waves surging across an open sea.

This complex region, however, tells an epic story. The flat fields of sugar beets, potatoes, and soybeans that stretch along the Minnesota border occupy what was the western shore of Glacial Lake Agassiz, an immense body of water that for millennia stood trapped between a wall of ice to the north and a single moraine far to the south. Prehistoric sand deltas that formed off Agassiz's shore can still be found in the sandhill prairies south of Fargo and under the thick, steeply rolling aspen forests southeast of Walhalla.

The full bulldozing power of a continental glacier on the move is evident throughout this region: In the high rolling hills south of Devils Lake on the state's east-central drift plain, on the wooded slopes and steep-sided lakes of the Turtle Mountains (where buried ice lingered

LEFT: *Creamy white narrow-leaved poisonvetch punctuates a rolling mixed-grass prairie at the Lostwood National Wildlife Refuge. Federally endangered piping plover frequent the shores of the distant lake.*

for centuries after the rest of the glacier had disappeared), in the high pothole-riddled rangeland of the Missouri Coteau. The scarps that tower above the free-running waters of the Pembina River in the state's northeastern corner still bear witness to the massive power of ancient meltwater rivers at full flood. Even the 350-mile path of the Missouri River is a glacial consequence: Its curving course marks the southernmost advance of the last great ice sheet.

Once encompassing nearly four million acres of wetlands and prairie—tallgrass on the lake plain, mid-grass to the west—the grasslands east and north of the Missouri were home to wolves, huge herds of elk, bison, and pronghorn, and flocks of ducks, geese, and shorebirds. The big animals are gone now, along with all the tallgrass and most of the mid-grass prairie. Although more than half of the wetlands have been drained or filled, the hundreds of thousands of waterfowl that crowd the remaining oases give a sense of the abundant wildlife that these prairies sustained for millennia.

This chapter begins in the state's southeastern corner near Fargo, in the sandhills of the Sheyenne Grassland, and proceeds west along the South Dakota border onto the Missouri Coteau. Winding through a rolling terrain punctuated with pothole lakes and wildlife refuges, it heads north to the Devils Lake region and then to Pembina Gorge, northwest of Walhalla. The journey concludes with a swing west across the top of the state to visit the Turtle Mountains and a number of federal wildlife refuges in the Souris River basin, culminating at Lostwood, a crown jewel of the refuge system west of Kenmare.

ABOVE: *In full display on its spring mating ground with a purple neck sac and yellow eye comb, a sharp-tailed grouse joins other males at dawn to stake out territories with foot-stomping and odd vocalizations.*

OVERLEAF: *In southeast North Dakota, cottonwoods in the Sheyenne Sandhills catch the morning light. This rolling, starkly beautiful region harbors the last significant remnant of tallgrass prairie in the state.*

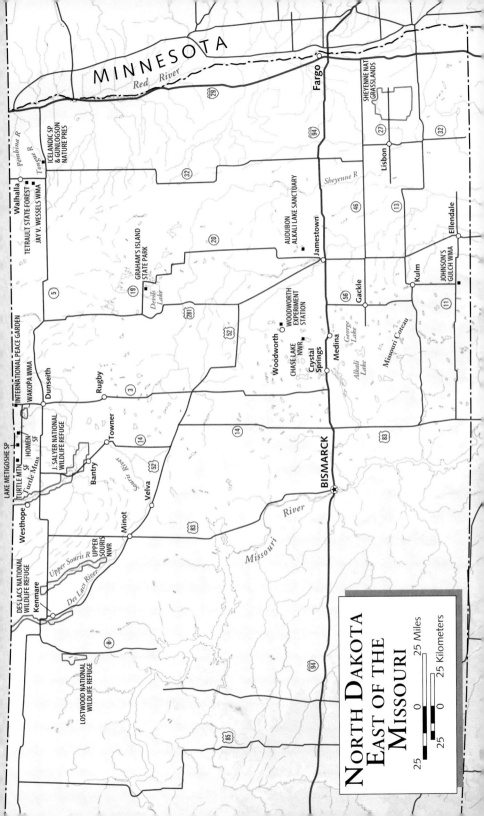

NORTH DAKOTA
EAST OF THE
MISSOURI

25 Miles
0   25

25 Kilometers
0   25

THE GLACIATED PLAINS: SANDHILLS AND GRASSLANDS

About 30 miles southwest of Fargo lie the remains of the great tallgrass prairie that once commanded the eastern end of North Dakota. A vestige of a world now lost, the **Sheyenne Sandhills** encompass the largest single block of intact tallgrass prairie in the country outside eastern Kansas. Covering some 135,000 acres of rolling grassland, choppy sand prairie, and wooded savanna, the sandhills surround the lower reaches of the narrow, twisting Sheyenne River. More than half of the area is federally owned, the rest private ranchland. In the mid-1930s, in the darkest days of the depression and drought, Congress passed the Bankhead-Jones Farm Tenant Act, which empowered the federal government to buy some 70,000 acres of this handsome country from the unfortunate farmers who thought they could profitably plow these sandy hills. Now restored and administered by the U.S. Forest Service, the **Sheyenne National Grasslands❖** are managed both as rangeland leased to local ranchers and as a recreational area open to the public.

The sandhills are only a portion of a much larger sand delta laid down by the forerunner of the current Sheyenne River in the waning millennia of the last glacial retreat. At that time, the prehistoric Sheyenne ran broad and deep, swollen with meltwater and sand from the rotting ice sheet to the north. Here at its mouth, the river ended its journey, slipping quietly beneath the surface of now-extinct Glacial Lake Agassiz, which lay pooled between the ice front to the north and a high moraine to the south. By the time Agassiz had drained away and the old Sheyenne all but dried up, the river had built a 450,000-acre sand delta 75 feet thick in places. The centuries of drought that followed transformed the area into a dunescape, which was constantly worked and reworked by the wind before rain and vegetation returned.

Light soils and native grasses shimmering distinctively in the sunlight inspired early European settlers to call this place the Silver Prairie. Today, as then, the biologically rich sandhills support a number of habitats: open, gently rolling tallgrass and mixed-grass prairie in higher

LEFT: *While cover is often sparse for small mammals in the grasslands of the Sheyenne Sandhills, there's often safety underground. Here a pair of animal burrows probably shelters badgers or a den of coyotes.*

143

ABOVE: *Stretching unbroken to the horizon, a country road disappears over a ridge of rangeland on the Missouri Coteau west of Ellendale.*

areas, wet prairie in the swales, sedge meadows in the lowlands. Prairie grasses and flowers abound: big and little bluestem, Indian grass, and blue grama; goldenrods, tall blazing stars, torch flowers, leadplants, hairy puccoons, and white prairie asters. The state's largest population of greater prairie chickens inhabits the uplands. Moister areas support western prairie fringed orchids, and growing in the wet lowlands are prairie cordgrass and a variety of bulrushes, sedges, and cattails.

On the driest uplands, choppy grass-covered sand dunes are pocked with blowouts—steep sandy troughs where small colonies of cliff swallows have burrowed holes and made nests in the higher walls. Sandhill bluestem, spiderwort, hairy grama, and blowout grasses thrive here. Nearby, parklike clumps of stunted bur oak, cottonwood, aspen, and willow interrupt the hummocky, grassy savanna, and chokecherry, wild plum, and smooth sumac populate more protected areas. Sharp-tailed grouse hide in the tangled buckbrush and wood rose.

Along the river's terraces curl old channels of the Sheyenne, oxbows left high but not quite dry. Drainage, in fact, is poor enough to create conditions congenial to elm and basswood—species common much farther east—as well as green ash, cottonwood, and peachleaf willow. A search of the forest floor may yield such Great Lakes woodland wildflowers as bloodroot, jack-in-the-pulpit, nodding trillium, and Solomon's seal. Numerous springs and seeps at the base of some of the old oxbow terraces have created a genuine peatland, low places choked with alder and bog birch and extensive enough to sus-

ABOVE: *Wild turkeys forage near Johnson's Gulch. The area's wooded coulees provide ideal habitat for this fowl, which favors forest edges.*

tain moose. More than 800 plant species grow in these hills, which offer some of the best birding in the state.

Many of these habitats are preserved within three state wildlife management areas known as the **Mirror Pool Units.** Visitors can tour these beautiful public lands by car (which must remain on the two-track and gravel roads) or range more widely on foot or horseback. A grassland map, essential for a productive visit, is available at the Sheyenne Ranger District office in nearby Lisbon, at the junction of Routes 32 and 27.

Some 60 miles west—and a world away—is the high flank of the Missouri Coteau, the astonishing pile of debris left by a succession of glaciers and a looming reminder of the millennial forces that shaped this region. Its western edge forming the east bank of the Missouri River, the huge highland traverses the state, roughly paralleling the course of the river.

Although numerous roads ascend the Missouri Coteau from the east, only a few provide a good sense of the immense mass of the great moraine. One such highway is Route 11, which climbs the coteau some 15 miles west of Ellendale. Here the road runs along the north side of Johnson's Gulch, the largest and best known of numerous ravines that cut into the plateau's eastern flank. Southeast of the junction of Routes 11 and 56, the North Dakota Game and Fish Department has established the 1,400-acre **Johnson's Gulch Wildlife Management Area❖.** Deep and heavily wooded, the gulch extends well back into the

145

coteau, cut by numerous draws and supporting prairie on its uplands. The habitats in the gulch and along its ravines are typical of the multitude of wooded draws that once climbed over the eastern flanks of the coteau. Augmenting the property is the adjoining **Lazy M,** a 1,760-acre federal waterfowl production area (WPA). With its undulating, pothole-speckled prairie to the west and northwest, the Lazy M is managed primarily for ducks and geese.

A spring-fed creek winds through the gulch and courses down its floor. American elm dominates the bottomland here, and bur oak and green ash climb the grassy upper slopes. Humans have lived here for at least 2,000 years, and burial mounds date from before 100 B.C. Just prior to European settlement, the gulch was home to a band of Cut-head Sioux. The ravine was once a "buffalo jump," so called because bison driven over the gulch's steep north slope were slaughtered where they fell. Today bison bones still appear in eroding creek banks at the ravine's bottom.

ABOVE: *Among the continent's most populous ducks, northern pintail "dabble," or feed, in the area's shallow lakes; they nest in upland grasses.*

RIGHT: *In central North Dakota, farm fields surround the prairie potholes that provide breeding grounds for millions of migratory birds— the fabled "duck factory."*

THE MISSOURI COTEAU, POTHOLE PRAIRIES, AND ALKALINE LAKES

The rumpled, pothole-perforated grassland west of Johnson's Gulch is one of several large areas scattered across the coteau that are managed for waterfowl by the U.S. Fish and Wildlife Service. In this four-county area alone, the federal government owns more than 44,000 acres, and easement agreements with private landowners protect another 102,000 acres of wetlands. This **Kulm Wetland Management District**❖ also oversees three refuges on private lands. The federally owned tracts are open to hunting and trapping in season and to birders and hikers as well. Wildlife is abundant because the high grassland and rolling prairie here are blessed with water—from

freshwater seeps, fens, and cattail and bulrush marshes to permanent lakes, seasonal pools, and temporary wet spots. Before venturing out, be sure to get maps and information at district headquarters in Kulm at the junction of Routes 56 and 13.

Although a great deal of water pools on this huge pile of glacial debris, the region has amazingly few rivers. Not enough time has elapsed since the ice departed for streams to develop on this chaotic highland. Nevertheless, the coteau's thousands of marshes, lakes, ponds, and fens form a bafflingly interrelated hydrologic system. Constantly on the move, groundwater flows among lakes, potholes, and marshes. Because the water's chemical composition, particularly the salinity, varies from year to year, different wetlands support different wildlife at different times. On the coteau, freshwater marshes clothed in cattails and bulrushes and teeming with fathead minnows may lie cheek by jowl with barren fishless pools rimmed with salt and more saline than the sea.

A traveler in these parts can often "read" the landscape by noting what plants are growing around the potholes and what kinds of birds are in residence. When cattails and bulrushes appear along with scaup, mallard, pintail, shovelers, and teal, springs or seeps are probably feeding a freshwater pond that is sending its water percolating to wetlands downslope. Where only bulrushes crowd a shore or where concentrations of canvasbacks, wigeon, and, in the fall, tundra swans cruise beds of sago pondweed or widgeon grass, chances are the

148

LEFT: *A pair of alert white-tailed deer pause to check their surroundings at Chase Lake National Wildlife Refuge.*
RIGHT: *Near Chase Lake red fox kits, awaiting a parental food delivery, explore beyond their den; at four months they will be on their own.*

water is much saltier. In such transitional areas, waters are moving through from wetlands upslope to others lower in the basin. Where redheads and wigeon bob in bare potholes surrounded by salt, the wetland is probably a sink; the water it receives from all around can escape only by evaporation.

Running the gamut from permanent lakes and marshes to semipermanent pools, these wetlands also vary in the profusion of aquatic life they support. Freshwater ponds and seeps of saline lakes teem with hundreds of species of algae, amphipods, freshwater snails, and fairy shrimp; saltier waters attract clouds of brine flies and large populations of water boatmen, salt-tolerant snails, and brine shrimp. These tiny creatures are vital food sources for the millions of breeding and brooding waterfowl and shorebirds in these areas.

South of I-94 near Crystal Springs are two particularly interesting saline lakes. Some 20 miles west of the town of Gackle on Route 46, aptly named **Alkali Lake❖** spreads across a treeless basin. Because it produces an extensive crop of sago pondweed, the lake attracts large numbers of canvasback ducks and tundra swans among other species. **George Lake❖,** a few miles to the north, is a noted gathering place for large flocks of redhead ducks attracted by the lake's abundant stands of widgeon grass. Created when a buried glacial ice block melted under the rock debris atop it, deep George Lake is loaded with brine shrimp and water boatmen, rich protein sources for the waterfowl. Depending on weather and annual rainfall, the best time to see birds at both lakes is fall, usually October. Before planning a visit, check with the state's Game and Fish Department in Bismarck for specific conditions.

A particularly important center for waterfowl on the Missouri edge

149

ABOVE: *Annually, millions of ducks migrate to and breed in the shallow ponds of the Missouri Coteau, including such colorful species as (clockwise from top left) shovelers, lesser scaup, redheads, and blue-winged teal.*

of the Coteau, **Chase Lake National Wildlife Refuge❖** is north of I-94, about 16 miles northwest of Medina. Forming the center of a 4,385-acre refuge, the large, highly saline prairie lake is encircled by rolling uplands and a profusion of small ponds and marshy wetlands. Managed for waterfowl, the lake and variety of nearby wetlands attract huge numbers of migrating ducks, geese, and shorebirds. Federally endangered piping plover can be seen here, as well as Baird's sparrows, Sprague's pipits, and other uncommon species. Clumps of cattails around the lake's otherwise bare shores mark the springs and seeps that provide essential fresh water for ducklings, which would die without it. (All ducks possess salt glands to process ingested salts, but the glands do not become fully functional in ducklings until the sixth day after hatching.) The primary attractions at Chase, however, are the thousands of nesting white pelicans, gulls, and cormorants that flock to two large islands in the middle of the lake. From mid-April to late July, these waters are home to the largest nesting colony of white

150

ABOVE: *Green leafy cattails indicate that the waters of this marsh in the Chase Lake refuge are fresh and probably fed by springs, making it ideal for blue-winged teal, which favor such semipermanent wetlands.*

pelicans on the continent, a breeding population numbering between 10,000 and 12,000 birds. The refuge manager at the **Woodworth Waterfowl Production Area,** just east of the nearby town of Woodworth, can provide self-guided tour brochures and advice about the best time to observe specific species.

Before European settlement, the lowlands east of the Missouri Coteau accounted for most of North Dakota's share of the prairie pothole region. More than half have since been drained, and those wetlands that are left survive as pockets of species-rich habitat in a sea of industrial aquaculture. To experience one of these special places, take Route 20 north from Jamestown to the eight-mile marker and turn east for four miles. Owned by the National Audubon Society, the 2,200-acre **Alkali Lake Sanctuary**❖ is a model of how wildlife and agriculture can coexist. Purchased by the society from a number of surrounding farms, the site today is a rich mix of habitats: small wetlands, woods, prairie, and grass uplands. Once heavily grazed, the land has been returned to its natural state of prairie and wetlands. The wooded 500-acre lake, a central feature of the sanctuary, supports nesting habitat for waterfowl and serves as a staging area for spectacular numbers of migrating snow geese, tundra swans, and Canada geese. Wildlife here is profuse, including three kinds of rail, sharp-tailed grouse, longspurs, cuckoos, yellowlegs, white pelicans, wood ducks, both orchard and northern orioles, mink, beavers, and coyotes. A telephone call before visiting is advisable, and the sanctuary manager can provide information about prairie ecology, species biology, and wetland issues.

Continue north on Route 20 for about 85 miles to reach another rich birding area. Huge **Devils Lake❖** is not only the largest of several saline lakes in the area but also the biggest natural lake in the state. Despite considerable development, the lake supports a wealth of bird species. During spring and fall migration and nesting season, a four-mile stretch of marshes, meadows, and mudflats attracts an astonishing number of shorebirds to **Minnewaukan Flats❖,** at the southwestern end of the lake about four miles due east of Minnewaukan. A good year at Devils Lake brings tens of thousands of stilt sandpipers, long-billed dowitchers, American avocets, and semipalmated sandpipers. (Because what can be seen depends on seasonal conditions, visitors are advised to call in advance.) A classic closed basin, Devils Lake receives water from all around but has no outlet. Gouged out of the plain by the last advancing glacier—the hills to the south of the lake are the piled-up displaced earth—the big lake's volume is dictated by rainfall and seasonal rates of evaporation. Lake levels are constantly rising and falling—fluctuations now exaggerated because many of the surrounding wetlands, which once contained substantial amounts of water, have been drained. In wet years the flats can be inundated. Farther east and south are other excellent birding areas, including **Grahams Island State Park❖** and **Sullys Hill National Game Preserve❖.**

PEMBINA GORGE AND THE TURTLE MOUNTAINS

Northeast and northwest of the Devils Lake region lie two biologically rich landscapes that defiantly contradict the flat, treeless image of this state: the Pembina Gorge and the Turtle Mountains. The central feature of spectacular **Pembina Gorge❖** is the steep valley of the Pembina River. Rising in Manitoba and running east across the northeastern

ABOVE: *Winding south from Canada, the Pembina River crosses Tetrault Woods State Forest near Walhalla. Forests of oak, aspen, and birch, as well as marshes, and grasslands have made this area biologically rich.*

corner of North Dakota, the Pembina has cut a deep and dramatic ravine through the soft Cretaceous shale underlying this region. Once a channel carrying suddenly released meltwater from the glacial lakes to the west, the Pembina River valley is now the longest and deepest unaltered river valley in the state. Laid down some 90 million years ago, the dark shale that rises above the river is the oldest exposed rock in North Dakota, and the surrounding woodlands constitute one of the state's largest intact blocks of forest.

Scattered throughout this wooded valley is a patchwork of small prairies, wetlands, and shrub lands that together contain some of the greatest plant and animal diversity in the state. More than 75 species of breeding birds are found here, including 11 of North Dakota's 14 resident wood warblers, and upward of 480 different kinds of plants—one-third of the state's resident species—have been identified. The valley also supports the largest population of moose in North Dakota, and its only naturally occurring population of Manitoban elk.

Winding through the bottom of the valley is the Pembina, a particularly scenic canoe river. Although there are no public facilities, public lands flank the river in scattered sections along both shores, from its upper reaches to its confluence with the Red River on the Minnesota border. A fine all-day canoe trip is possible from above the Pembina

153

In the Pembina Gorge, a birch woodland (right) covers a hillside, one of 14 natural communities in the area that shelter moose (above), bears, coyotes, and elk. Lynx (below) move south into the gorge region when food—especially its principal prey, snowshoe hares—becomes scarce in Canada.

River Bridge to a take-out point in **Tetrault Woods State Forest**❖ just south of Walhalla. For information about water levels, maps, and other aids, contact the North Dakota Forest Service's office in Walhalla or the Game and Fish Department office in Devils Lake.

South and west of Walhalla, several other natural areas manifest the biological diversity of this region. **Jay V. Wessels Wildlife Management Area**❖ (named for a local game warden and conservationist) is a thickly wooded 3,383-acre dune field about seven miles south of Walhalla off Route 32. This sand is derived from delta deposits formed during Pleistocene times where an ancient river emptied into Glacial Lake Agassiz. Numerous undeveloped trails meander through dense forests of aspen and oak. Because the water table is high under the sand hills, conditions in low areas have created two large wetland bogs that are extensive enough to support moose and elk.

A few miles east of Jay Wessels on Route 5, **Gunlogson Nature Preserve** is a small gem of riparian habitat. Once part of a homestead owned by the Gunlogson family, the 200-acre preserve lies along a three-quarter-mile stretch of the Tongue River in the middle of **Icelandic State Park**❖. Self-guided nature trails wind through an oak and basswood forest within the preserve and beside shallow ponds and marshes adjacent to the river. Among the more than a dozen species considered threatened or rare in North Dakota are bishop's cap, crested woodfern, graceful sedge, and southern watermeal, one of the world's smallest flowering plants.

A hundred miles due west on Route 5, the second outstanding natural area of this northern region, the **Turtle Mountains**❖, rise from the surrounding treeless plain some 32 miles north of Rugby. The rumpled wooded hills, standing more than 600 feet above the flat floor of a long-extinct glacial lake, give travelers a visual jolt. Covered with a thick mantle of aspen and oak and dotted with lakes and marshes, this highland could be a landscape transported from north-central Minnesota. Once a large, isolated mesa of stacked sedimentary material standing above a flat plain, the "mountains"—extending about 44 miles east-west but only 25 miles north and south—do indeed resemble a turtle.

Successive glaciers from the north deposited atop the mesa thick layers of debris that insulated the ice below from warming temperatures and slowed its final disintegration. When the underlying ice finally melted, the debris on top collapsed, creating today's rugged roller-coaster terrain. Because they are taller than the surrounding plain, the Turtles catch more rain and snow—enough in combination with other factors to support thick, diverse woodlands, a wealth of habitats, and an abundance of plant and animal species. Forests—bur oak in the coulees with aspen above—and grasslands climb the foothills to the steeply rolling uplands, which are covered in thick aspen and paper birch forest with American elm, green ash, and box elder mixed in. The whole area is riddled with lakes, ponds, marshes, and even a sphagnum bog.

One place encompassing all these elements is the 6,800-acre **Wakopa Wildlife Management Area✣,** just south of the Canadian border about eight miles east of the junction of Routes 281 and 43 north of Dunseith. Here the terrain is deeply rolling and thickly wooded. A profusion of steep-sided kettle lakes and marshes (serviced by 21.5 miles of foot trails) and small upland meadows dot the hummocky interior. Moose, deer, elk, and ruffed grouse inhabit the woods, as do lynx and their favored prey, snowshoe hares.

Some 22 miles west of Wakopa on Route 43 is **Lake Metigoshe State Park✣,** a 1,200-acre wooded tract in the heart of the hills. On the east side of the lake, the largest body of water in the Turtles, the park contains a thick forest of aspen and bur oak, as well as many marshes and kettle lakes. Habitats here support the full complement of wildlife found in these highlands, including moose, elk, beavers, mink, red foxes, and a number of other species. An extensive all-season trail system links the park and campgrounds, and the environmental learning center provides a variety of educational programs for groups that reserve ahead of time.

State forests manifest much of the area's biological diversity. About five miles west of Lake Metigoshe on Route 43 is **Turtle Mountain State Forest✣,** which comprises 7,494 acres around **Strawberry Lake,** a hub for migrating waterfowl. Some 45 miles of scenic trails lead visitors through thick aspen-oak forest to many small lakes and marshes. **Pelican** and **Sandy lakes,** two other excellent birding areas, are within 4,484-acre **Homen State Forest✣,** some six miles east of Lake Metigoshe; white pelicans, cormorants, pintail, and wood ducks are frequently spotted.

Straddling the U.S.–Canadian border off Route 3 in the middle of these highlands is the **International Peace Garden✣,** 2,300 acres of

forest, lakes, swamps, and marshes. Dedicated in 1932 to peace between the two nations, the formal garden is an exquisitely maintained affair in an otherwise natural landscape.

WILDLIFE REFUGES:
THE SOURIS BASIN AND LOSTWOOD

West of the Turtle Mountains lies an extensive river basin, a landscape dominated by a huge loop of the meandering Souris River. The French word for mouse, *souris*—the direct translation of the Native American name for this stream—commemorated the proliferation of mice once found in the surrounding meadows. The river began as a spillway for waters from a Canadian glacial lake in the vicinity of Regina. Rising in Saskatchewan, the Souris now enters North Dakota northwest of Minot, runs southeast as far as Velva, and then suddenly makes a U-turn, heads back to the northwest, and exits the state northeast of Westhope. On that return trip to Canada, it crosses the old bed of Glacial Lake Souris and the remnants of the large sandy delta left by the lake as it drained.

Early morning sun glints off dew drops that coat the web of an orb weaver spider (far left) in Lake Metigoshe State Park. Native flora and fauna here include a delicate wild columbine (left) and a wary eastern cottontail rabbit (above).

Flanking the Souris loop are three major national wildlife refuges. The westernmost—19,554-acre **Des Lacs National Wildlife Refuge**❖—brackets the Des Lacs River, a Souris tributary, and parallels the 32,000-acre **Upper Souris National Wildlife Refuge**❖ which is farther east along the southbound Upper Souris.

The third and most easterly sanctuary is the **J. Clark Salyer National Wildlife Refuge**❖, an outstanding preserve along the Souris's northbound stretch. Reached by Route 14 north from Towner, the 59,000-acre Salyer refuge occupies both sides of a 50-mile stretch of the river, essentially from Bantry to the Canadian border. The largest refuge in the state and one of the finest in the region, J. Clark Salyer shelters a variety of habitats, including hardwood bottomland forest dominated by elm and green ash; 20,000 acres of shallow marshlands; upland meadows; and an extensive sandhill prairie at its southern end—a grassy rolling

OVERLEAF: *In the Turtle Mountains near the Canadian border, the waters of School Section Lake in Lake Metigoshe State Park mirror a rippled sky and a wooded shoreline of quaking aspens and beaked hazelnut trees.*

Left: *An American avocet stalks insects and seeds in the shallow waters of an alkaline pothole. This shorebird feeds by sweeping its recurved bill across the mud or water surface.* **Right:** *High on the Missouri Coteau in northwest North Dakota, a prairie pothole sparkles under cumulus clouds and an intensely blue sky at the incomparable Lostwood refuge.*

dunescape supporting a patchy scrub forest of oak and aspen. Birding is excellent: Some 250 species of birds have been recorded here. More than a quarter of a million ducks live on or visit the refuge annually, and 300,000 snow geese use it as a staging area during their spring migration. Some 13 miles of the Souris are designated part of the National Trail System; upland paths connect different parts of the refuge, including the drumming sites of ruffed grouse. A 22-mile seasonal auto tour also winds through most of the refuge's representative habitats.

West of the Souris loop refuges and 16 miles west of Kenmare on Route 8 is a fourth federal holding, a crown jewel of the National Wildlife Refuge System. Straddling a high crest of the Missouri Coteau, **Lostwood National Wildlife Refuge**❖ encompasses a breathtaking expanse of wildly rolling, pothole-riddled short-grass and mixed-grass prairie. Lostwood is particularly distinguished because about 70 percent of its 26,900 acres is virgin prairie, landscape that was here 200 years ago. Although the bison, grizzlies, plains wolves, and pronghorn (once called American antelope) are gone—along with colossal numbers of waterfowl and shorebirds—this remnant of original prairie endures. On the uplands sharp-tailed grouse, Baird's sparrows, Sprague's pipits, and upland sandpipers coexist with badgers, coyotes, weasels, and jackrabbits. Salt-rimmed ponds and small lakes in low areas harbor all manner of prairie birds: gadwalls, wigeon, blue-winged teal, scaup, marbled godwits, American avocets, Wilson's phalaropes, piping plover, Virginia rails. Red-tailed and Swainson's hawks glide overhead; northern harriers and short-eared owls work the low grassy swales. Both great horned and long-eared owls are nocturnal hunters. A five-mile hiking trail winds through the rolling uplands, and a seven-mile self-guided auto tour also traverses a portion of the refuge.

WEST OF THE MISSOURI:
BUTTES AND BADLANDS

West of the Missouri River, ruggedly beautiful southwestern North Dakota was fashioned by far older—and far more relentless—forces than the glaciers that bulldozed the terrain farther east. Dominating the western reaches of the state are the badlands of the Little Missouri River, a broken, uneven landscape of breathtaking vistas, deep coulees, colorful scarps, and fabulously eroded buttes. Assembled from ancient material washed from the flanks of the emerging Rocky Mountains farther west, this region is composed of soft sands, silts, and clays that broad rivers deposited in swamps and marshes some 57 to 55 million years ago.

Although the sculpting of the badlands probably began 40 million years ago, serious erosion did not occur until about 600,000 years ago, when the first glacier arrived. Coming to rest east of the north-flowing Little Missouri, the massive wall of ice diverted all the rivers in the area south along its leading edge. In doing so, the glacier shaped the course of the modern Missouri River and also triggered the intensive erosion that continues today in the Little Missouri River basin.

Besides the obvious scenic splendor of the badlands, this region is a place of quiet beauty and abundant wildlife, where gently rolling, prairie-covered hills and broad valleys laced by rivers and woody draws support a surprising assemblage of biological diversity. Visitors

---

LEFT: *On the Cross Ranch preserve, a glacial boulder lies exposed on a grassy hill near the Missouri River. When explorers Lewis and Clark arrived here in 1804, they found Mandan and Hidatsa villages nearby.*

often experience profound awe at the simplicity of the solitary buttes that tower over open plains. Lone survivors of a vanished landscape, these rocky remnants are stark reminders of how much of the primordial land has worn away.

Much has changed here in just the past 200 years. When Lewis and Clark passed through this region on their epic journey up the Missouri

at the beginning of the nineteenth century, they wrote about great herds of bison and pronghorn in the valleys on the uplands, the abundance of elk and wolves, and, in the bottomlands, the grizzly bears. When North Dakota became a state in 1889, the bison, elk, and grizzlies had largely disappeared, but the river was still an unimpeded 360-mile stream threading its way among islands cloaked each autumn with golden cottonwoods. It lapped against sandy cutbanks and rushed around and over sandbar shallows and gravel spits. In places dense floodplain forests—cottonwood, green ash, elm, box elder—bracketed its course. Open prairie descended to the river down steep hills creased by wooded draws that wandered back into the uplands. Alternately flooding in spring and shrinking to a narrowed main channel flanked by shallow braided streams in summer, the Missouri changed from year to year, constantly shifting its bed and with it the attendant habitats that flourished in the bottomlands. Still the commanding presence of the region, the river today is dammed, tamed, and impounded. In North Dakota, the largest impoundment is giant Lake Sakakawea.

ABOVE: *Each June prairie roses, the state flower, fleck the green grasslands with splashes of vivid pink; the scarlet fruits remain on the bush into winter.*

This chapter starts beside the Missouri River about 20 miles north of Bismarck in a preserve that looks much as it did two centuries ago. Next it follows I-94 west to Medora and the South Unit of Theodore Roosevelt National Park. After ranging north and south on forest roads

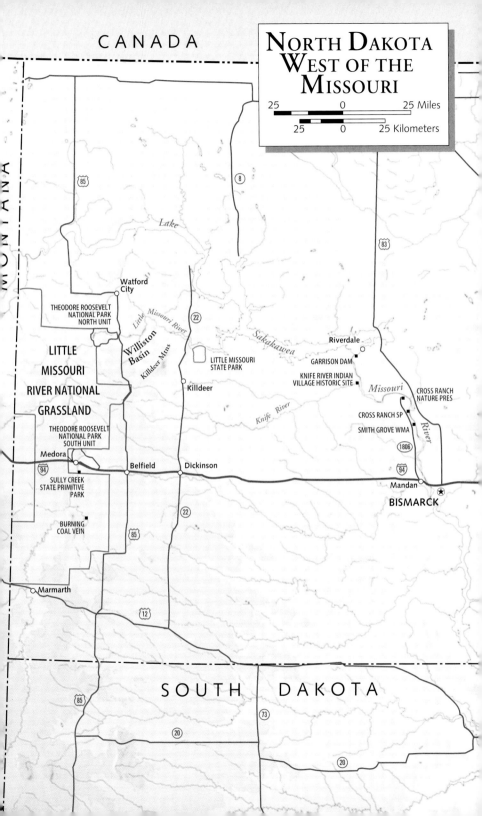

ABOVE: *World-class clouds scud across the sky above the broad Missouri River at Cross Ranch State Park. In his diary William Clark de-*

through the Little Missouri National Grassland, the itinerary concludes in the Killdeer Mountains east of the North Unit of Theodore Roosevelt National Park.

ALONG THE BANKS OF THE MISSOURI

Today nearly 90 percent of the once free-flowing Missouri River in North Dakota is a giant lake impounded by the earth-and-concrete Garrison Dam near Riverdale and the earthen bulk of the Oahe Dam just north of Pierre, South Dakota. Barely 45 miles of river still roll free through a landscape that still looks—at least superficially—like the wildlife-rich river valley that sustained Native Americans for centuries and inspired the descriptions of early explorers. On the stretch running south from the Garrison Dam to Bismarck, however, is a place missed by ravaging progress, where the Missouri flows through a land that appears little changed from the late October day in 1804 when Lewis and Clark described the view.

Some 23 miles north of Bismarck on Route 1806, the 6,000-acre **Cross Ranch Nature Preserve❖** and adjacent 560-acre **Cross Ranch State Park❖** are strung along the river's western bank. Encompassing the largest intact tract of Missouri River floodplain forest in the state, the preserve is backed to the west by what Meriwether Lewis called "hand-

scribed how the Hidatsa burned the nearby hills each spring to encourage an early crop of grass, "an enducement for the buffalow to feed on."

some, high steep prairie"—hills ascending to an open mixed-grass prairie. Stands of bur oak, ash, and aspen choke the wooded coulees, and brushy gullies thread their way through the hills to the treeless plain above. Owned by the Nature Conservancy, the preserve maintains a herd of about a hundred bison, which range into the hills.

In the southern reaches of the ranch, yucca and ball cactus cover precipitous south-facing hillsides while northern uplands support a small cluster of wetlands. Streams descending the coulees sustain beavers; other wildlife here includes wild turkeys and burrowing owls, bobcat, coyotes, red foxes, and both white-tailed and mule deer. Overhead sharp-shinned, Swainson's, and red-tailed hawks join the occasional bald eagle scouting for prey below. Along with Say's phoebes and chestnut-collared longspurs, rarer birds appear as well. In past years, migrating whooping cranes have stopped here, and least terns and piping plover have nested on sandbars. Within the forested lowlands along the river's terraces, large numbers of songbirds nest. In all, some 100 species of birds have been recorded here and more than 300 species of plants. Roughly 16 miles of hiking and cross-country ski trails wander through the preserve, which also features burial mounds and rock effigies, eagle trapping pits, and other sites that testify to human occupation as long ago as 6,000 years.

LEFT: *A pair of burrowing owls keeps watch above their nest, typically an abandoned rodent burrow that the birds commandeer and then adapt.*

RIGHT: *Before the Missouri was dammed, broad stands of cottonwoods laced the bottomlands. At Cross Ranch State Park, this grove persists.*

Indeed, this stretch of river and the land immediately to the north are extremely rich in human history. A longtime center of Mandan and Hidatsa society, this area was also a winter layover site for Lewis and Clark on their way west. Today **Fort Mandan,** a reproduction of the rough-hewn compound they built, commands the eastern bank of the Missouri where it curves west just a few miles north of the preserve. (The real fort was washed away by the shifting Missouri a few years after it was erected.) Upstream, at the confluence of the Knife and Missouri, the **Knife River Indian Villages National Historic Site**❖ contains a 1,758-acre tract of bottomland forest and mid-grass prairie. Here three Hidatsa villages give visitors a rare chance to study what life was like along the Missouri before white settlement.

Four miles south of Cross Ranch headquarters, a 23-acre grove of magnificent cottonwood trees occupies a river terrace in **Smith Grove Wildlife Management Area**❖. Estimated to be 250 to 300 years old, 12 of the cottonwoods are more than 15 feet in circumference and 90 to 100 feet tall. Unusually large in any age, some of these trees were a century old when Lewis and Clark traveled through the area.

THEODORE ROOSEVELT NATIONAL PARK

Visitors following I-94 from Mandan west to the badlands in North Dakota's southwestern corner find few hints of the extraordinary landscape that awaits them. Some seven miles beyond Belfield, the flat to gently rolling rangeland suddenly opens up to reveal a wild Technicolor canyonland. The badlands of the Little Missouri River—a vast expanse of gullied country some 120 miles in length and 34 miles across—border most of the last 280 river miles of the Little Missouri. Inscribed on the brightly colored, banded faces of these bluffs, ridges, pinnacles, and buttes—and on the canyon walls—are 55 to 60 million years of history.

Theodore Roosevelt (right) came to North Dakota in 1883 and as a young rancher honed many of his far-sighted conservationist ideas. A national park named for him now preserves superb badland terrain including the South Unit's Painted Canyon (left).

The centerpiece of the region is **Theodore Roosevelt National Park❖,** named for the twenty-sixth president, who arrived to hunt bison in 1883 and promptly fell in love with what he called "this land of vast silent spaces." Roosevelt later owned two cattle ranches in the area (the undeveloped Elkhorn Ranch, about 35 miles north, and the Maltese Cross, 7 miles south) and became an ardent conservationist. Believing that his visits to the badlands strengthened his mind as well as a body weakened by a sickly childhood, he declared, "I could not have been President had it not been for my experience in North Dakota."

The park is spread over 70,447 acres; the **North Unit** encompasses a dramatic bend in the river some 70 miles north of the **South Unit,** which is off I-94 near Medora. The 218-acre Elkhorn Ranch Site lies between the North and South units along the Little Missouri River. The three sections fall within the **Little Missouri National Grassland❖,** more than a million acres of federal land extending along both sides of the river and riddled with private inholdings, mostly ranches.

The river, the park, and the badlands all lie within the Williston Basin, a shallow 200,000-square-mile depression that formed in the continental crust half a billion years ago. Beginning with the violent birth of the Rockies 65 million years ago, successive episodes of mountain building sent myriad layers of sediment into the basin, where it hardened into rock. When the Rockies took a final heave upward some 12 million years ago, western North Dakota tilted east, causing its north- and east-flowing rivers to cut into the layers of sedimentary rock. The arrival of the glaciers accelerated the process, forcing the Little Missouri eastward over a shorter, steeper course. Up and down the valley, collapsing soft sediments fell away in a gully-carving cycle that continues today as rain, snow, seeps, and streams erode the landscape.

173

ABOVE: *In the park's South Unit a dark seam of lignite coal (left) divides a bed of gray bentonite. Lignite often ignites spontaneously, baking the surrounding clays into layers of hard, red-tinted clinker (right).*

The consequences are most colorfully exposed in the **Painted Canyon** of the the park's **South Unit,** a phantasmagoric land of vividly banded buttes, knobs, pillars, benches, and winding mini-canyons and coulees. Fluted, rumpled slopes of khaki-colored clay and siltstone are evidence of deposits along an ancient river, which became the floor of a vast open swamp. A brown sandstone scarp capped in burnt sienna suggests the sea level rose, leaving marine sediments above older materials. Washed in bands of gray and yellow-browns and streaked with black, a decaying knob of deeply creased claystone bespeaks a succession of landscapes dominated by open swamps and tropical forest.

The work not of rivers but of rain, erosion here has proceeded at very irregular rates, accelerating during droughts when the protective vegetative cover disappears. The varying hardness of clay, shale, and sandstone also determines how fast each wears away. Porous rock absorbs rains and snowmelt, slowing erosion, while impermeable rock of the same hardness erodes more rapidly. Particularly malleable are the bentonitic clays, which originated as volcanic ash blown and washed in

LEFT: *A bison drinks at a water hole in the South Unit. In 1956, 29 bison were reintroduced into the park; the herd now numbers nearly 300.*

OVERLEAF: *An overlook in the park's North Unit affords a fine panorama of the Little Missouri River and its spectacularly eroded valley.*

from the west. Composed of extremely fine particles, these clays swell when wet, absorbing up to five times their weight in water. When eroded by running water, bentonite becomes a slick, clinging muck that makes travel impossible.

Many of the bright colors in the badlands result from lignite seams running laterally through the ancient sediments. Easily ignited by lightning or spontaneous combustion, lignite burns fiercely, although in a slow process, and it bakes the rocks above it, turning hillsides into brick. Called clinker, these cooked clays, shales, and sandstones turn a riot of colors—red, gray, black, purple, yellow. (Here baked rock is usually red because the area is rich in iron oxide.) Often more resistant than clays and sandstones, clinker frequently becomes the red caprock atop pillars of eroded softer rock; it is also the local road-building material of choice, often incorrectly called scoria.

A major feature of the park's South Unit is the 36-mile self-guided auto tour, which leads to a variety of scenic viewpoints and for a closer look, hiking trails. The tour begins at the visitor center near Medora, where the rustic Maltese Cross cabin from Roosevelt's first ranch has been relocated. Beyond the Medora Overlook is a prairie-dog town whose residents bark warnings to announce the approach of visitors. The River Woodland Overlook affords a view of the Little Missouri River, flanked by stately cottonwoods and bordered by a rainbow of wildflowers in the spring (early autumn is also a good time for wildflower aficionados). Yucca, cacti, evening star, sego lilies, leopard lilies, and bluebells bloom in the park throughout the growing season.

A couple of hiking trails beckon along the auto tour. The Jones Creek Trail at Mile 21, which follows an eroded creekbed, offers a good chance to see wildlife. The park shelters small herds of reintroduced bison numbering between 250 and 400 head, as well as elk,

bighorn sheep, wild horses, and mule deer. Golden eagles soar above, rattlesnakes bask on rocks, and many species of songbirds range through the hills including mountain bluebirds in the spring. The steep Wind Canyon Trail affords a spectacular view of a curve in the Little Missouri and the strange shapes the wind has carved by blowing sand into the canyon on the left.

Where the park's South Unit dazzles with its vibrant colors, the less frequently visited **North Unit,** about 52 miles north of Belfield on Route 85, overwhelms with its sweeping views of the Little Missouri River and the eerie, broken land around it. Odd knobs, bizarre slab-capped pillars, and scattered stone "mushrooms" abound here, and littering the ground are hard cannonball-shaped spheres of clay and concretions of all shapes and sizes: round, elliptical, cylindrical, and irregular. These strange objects are the work of wind and water in different combinations; the harder sandstones are more resistant to erosion than the softer clays.

Among the highlights of the North Unit along a 30-mile auto tour are the Squaw Creek Nature Trail, where a leaflet shows visitors many of the plants used by the Plains Indians; the River Bend Overlook, which provides a fine panorama of the river valley and badlands; the Man and Grass Pullout, where grasslands are still visible; and the stunning Oxbow Overlook.

BUTTES, PLATEAUS, AND BADLANDS

For those willing to rough it, an excellent base for exploring the country in and around **Theodore Roosevelt National Park** is **Sully Creek**

LEFT: *Junipers dot the terrain near the Burning Coal Vein. Normally bushlike, the conifers are columnar here due to sulphuric fumes from the lignite.*

RIGHT: *The lavender narrowleaf penstemon, well-adapted to dry, rocky ground, is a common summertime sight in the North Dakota badlands.*

State Primitive Park❖, a few miles south of Medora. Located off Forest Road (FH) 3 on a scenic bend of the Little Missouri River, Sully Creek provides primitive camping as well as a corral for visitors who bring their own horses. A four-mile connecting trail for both horses and hikers leads to the national park. The campground also offers visitors easy access to the Little Missouri, a superb float and canoe river during the spring. To paddle the 110-mile stretch between Medora and the Long X Bridge on Route 85 just outside the national park's North Unit takes three to four days. Other stretches of the 274-mile river between Marmarth and its mouth are also canoeable, although there are only a few weeks when air temperatures and water depth (at least two feet) permit a pleasant, unimpeded run. Check with the park service at the South Unit.

Wild and rugged, the **Long X** is a 9,500-acre roadless area adjacent to the southern boundary of Theodore Roosevelt's North Unit just west of Route 85. Located in the McKenzie District of the **Little Missouri National Grassland❖,** Long X is one of four low-impact areas in that district where visitors are encouraged to hike and camp. It is also a tract that conservation organizations, the oil and gas industry, and the Forest Service have been wrangling over for years.

Visitors can hike or camp throughout the federal portions of the Little Missouri National Grassland. Well-maintained gravel roads, marked FH, extend the length of the badlands from south of the park's North Unit down to Marmarth, enabling visitors to experience the many dimensions of this spectacular country. Essential Forest Service maps of the region are available at both units of the park and at Forest Service offices in Watford City and Dickinson. The Forest Service also offers a map and brochure detailing an excellent 58-mile self-guided auto tour into the badlands south of Medora.

Despite the stark beauty and seeming wildness of these canyons and coulees, the landscape bears the marks of the twentieth century. Today the badlands are riddled with oil pumps, access roads, equipment sheds, and other facilities. Throughout the Little Missouri National Grassland, more than 540 oil wells, all with access roads, pump away. As recently as the early 1970s, a hiker could traverse the region between the park's two units without crossing a road, a feat now impossible. At that time, some 550,000 acres were roadless; today less than a quarter remain so.

One rare undeveloped tract is 21,120 acres of classic badlands surrounding the **Kinley Plateau,** a broken upland some 10 miles south of Medora on FH 3. Steep claystone buttes and intricately fluted slumps banded in taupes, beiges, ochers, and grays stand above low bench tops snowy-white with alkali. Shards of petrified wood and odd-shaped concretions rusty with iron oxide lie scattered on the ground, while red clinker ridges rise dramatically against the brilliant blue skyline. On the buttes are fractured slabs of hard sandstone. Below, wooded, stream-fed coulees shaded by cottonwoods and green ashes and brushy draws lined with buckbrush, wild plum, chokecherry, and rabbitbrush disappear into a jumble of grass-, sage-, and juniper-covered hills. Although no facilities or developed trails aid explorers of the 11 archaeological and two historical sites here, the experience is unforgettable.

Kinley Plateau is one of several badlands areas that a consortium of North Dakota conservation groups is working to protect from oil and gas development. The industry, reluctant to close off areas that may contain petroleum, has mounted a stiff resistance.

The badlands are classic bighorn sheep country. Until 1993, when an illegal oil-access road was punched into its northwest corner, Kinley Plateau—together with Moody Plateau to the north and Cliffs Plateau to the south—supported the area's only established population of bighorns unaffected by oil and gas development. Now numbering about 65 animals, the group is one of several that the state has reintroduced into remote areas of the badlands in the last 25 years. The future of this ongoing project is unclear because increasing numbers of wells, roads, and vehicles are reducing the habitat of the transplanted populations as well as the possibility of finding suitably remote sites to place additional groups of bighorns.

To the southwest, just across FH 3, a range of hills and canyons descend to a coffee-and-cream-colored Little Missouri. Dominating the skyline across the river is massive flat-topped **Bullion Butte❖,** a sheer prairie-capped plateau that rises above rugged foothills. Also proposed for protection, the butte lies at the heart of a 19,130-acre expanse that combined with Kinley Plateau forms the largest tract of roadless land remaining in North Dakota. The roughly 60 bighorn sheep that now live in this remote area appear to be the only reproducing herd in this southern region. The best times to see bighorns in these hills are summer and fall, after the lambs are born. If ewes are disturbed during spring lambing, they will abandon their young, which then become sure prey for coyotes.

Continuing south, FH 3 wends its way under red clinker buttes and knobs and juniper-clad hills until it arrives unexpectedly at a startlingly out-of-place pine savanna. Stretching into the hills to the south, this area supports the state's only major stand of ponderosa pine, a species common in the Rocky Mountains. The nearest major ponderosa forest is found in South Dakota's Black Hills, some 185 miles south.

A mile west is **Burning Coal Vein❖,** an underground lignite seam that smoldered steadily for more than a century. Possibly ignited at an outcrop by lightning or a prairie fire, the seam burned slowly—about ten feet a year—because it received little oxygen. Although the fires at last appear to be out, they have left a distinctive landscape. As the underground lignite turned to ash, the grassy slope above collapsed into a series of tiered ridges that descend to the road.

To the south, downwind, sulfuric fumes from the burning lignite have caused the normally squat, conical Rocky Mountain junipers that climb the grassy clay and sandstone ridges to assume tall, columnar forms. In this remarkable and haunting landscape, the draws that lace the high grasslands contain the only nesting population of Audubon's warblers in the state. The best time to visit is early summer, when the birds flit about and wildflowers bloom against the red flanks of the clinker knobs.

THE NORTHERN LITTLE MISSOURI

More than 200 river miles north of these southern badlands lies the mouth of the Little Missouri. The smaller river, which once slipped into the wide channel of the mighty Missouri, now empties quietly into a backwater of impounded Lake Sakakawea. Presiding over this confluence is the finest of North Dakota's state parks. From the town of Killdeer take Route 22 north for 17 miles to a gravel road running 3 miles east to the park.

Little Missouri State Park❖ encompasses some 5,900 acres of exquisite canyons and coulees, dramatic buttes and plateaus, and rumpled prairie. When the north-flowing Little Missouri was forced eastward by glacial ice that blocked its natural drainage, it spilled over more steeply inclined terrain. As it gained speed, the river bit deeply into the soft clays underlying it, carving a trench more than 500 feet deep. The process of gullying all along the trench walls produced the distinctive, deeply fluted landscape that draws visitors here today.

In this stunning park, deep forested coulees wind into the rolling highlands, which are carpeted in wheatgrass, little bluestem, little rice grass, and silver sagebrush. Rocky Mountain juniper climbs the north-facing hills, and skunkbush, rabbitbrush, and buckbrush crowd a multitude of arroyos. On hot, dry south-facing slopes cacti, yucca, and sage predominate. The park is also home to a wealth of badlands wildlife such as both bald and golden eagles, prairie falcons, bobcat, coyotes, and mule deer. Cedar waxwings, rufous-sided towhees, flycatchers, and a host of other species nest in the brushy draws.

Horses offer an excellent way to explore this park. More than 30 miles of trails traverse a variety of terrains and habitats, and the park provides a horse corral, horse concession, and equestrian guides. Hiking is a good alternative, and the camping is primitive but wonderful.

Between the state park and the North Unit of Theodore Roosevelt rise the **Killdeer Mountains,** a 3,000-foot range of wooded hills that ascend some 700 feet from the flat plain above the Little Missouri River valley. The Killdeers are an impressive reminder that much of North Dakota has disappeared. These "mountains" were once two massive flat-topped plateaus that are now dissected into numerous fingerlike spurs alternating with deep wooded valleys. Their summit is rimmed by a towering palisade of broken, rocky outcrops. Water percolating through has eroded the rocks in interesting ways, carving coves and caves. **Medicine Cave,** a 70-foot-deep cavity hollowed out of limestone, is the largest and best known.

The rock that caps these plateaus is chiefly volcanic ash deposited

ABOVE: *A layer of orange clinker stains the rumpled landscape a rusty red at Little Missouri State Park; its dramatic topography and varied flora and fauna make the park the crown jewel of the state system.*

in large lakes here during the Miocene era. Blown on winds from the west, the ash originated in the Rockies, which were undergoing one of their extensive periods of vulcanism. Over millennia, the lakes dried up and the softer land around them eroded, leaving only the two "mountains" standing over the plain. If these plateaus once formed the bottom of lakes, the surrounding land must have been considerably higher. Between 5 and 3 million years ago—long before the first glaciers ground into the state—a mind-boggling amount of this portion of North Dakota must have washed away in what is known as an inversion of topography.

Prairie on the Killdeers' summit is home to a number of rare plants, among them tiny daisylike cushion fleabane. The southern slopes support prairie smoke, miner's candle, and Indian hemp. Extensive forest—the largest in this corner of the state—of oak, aspen, and paper birch cloaks the north-facing slopes, and spring-fed streams wind through the wooded valleys. Beavers have colonized the ponds along the pass, and at dawn or dusk, hikers often see mule deer or elk. Coyotes howl from the hills, and golden eagles, vultures, and hawks glide above.

SOUTH DAKOTA

PART THREE

SOUTH DAKOTA

Sprawled across the continent's midsection, South Dakota is a splendid patchwork of distinctive landscapes. Sweeping from east to west, green rolling range- and farmlands and high pothole-riddled plateaus give way to broad river basins. Undulating hills and dead-level plains of grass and sage follow in the arid country farther west, which is studded with steep, solitary buttes. In the far southwest, fantastical badlands, their pinnacles and fluted scarps sculpted by erosion, prepare the way for the Black Hills, which were named for the dark pines that cling to their rugged slopes.

Bisecting the state is the legendary Missouri River, the once-mighty waterway that for thousands of years sustained wildlife and native peoples and drew the first European explorers to the West. East of the Missouri, now dammed and converted into vast lakes, the rolling terrain owes much to the sculpting power of glacial ice. Along the state's eastern border, the effect of the last ice age has been profound. When the final glacier stalled on a highland here about 10,000 years ago and then stagnated as temperatures warmed, the debris insulated pockets of ice below. After the ice melted, the earth above collapsed into the cavities, creating an unusual terrain of steep hills peppered with innumerable lakes, pools, and ponds.

Eighteenth-century French explorers and trappers were the first Europeans to visit this region, naming it the Coteau des Prairies, or the prairie highland. In its marshes, lakes, and wetlands they found a landscape teeming with wildlife, particularly migrating waterfowl. This fertile wet prairie, however, was among the first places in South Dakota to fall under the hungry cutting edge of the plow. Today, corn, wheat, hay, barley, and cattle thrive where once seemingly infinite tallgrass prairie billowed before the wind. Most of the mid-grasses and wetlands, too, have vanished, replaced by an endless expanse of pasture and carefully cultivated farmland. Indeed, farms and ranches now occupy about 90 percent of South Dakota.

PRECEDING PAGES: *A summer sunset imparts a rosy glow to the rugged slumps and scarps of South Dakota's intensely scenic Badlands National Park. The name is derived from* mako sica, Lakota *for "land bad."*

For surveyors and pioneers moving west, the wide James River low-land marked the beginning of the northern plains. From here a rolling sea of grass stretched westward, up another prominent highland left by the final glacier, to the eastern shores of the Missouri. As the ice sheet disintegrated, debris accumulated along the river's eastern bank to form the great Missouri Coteau, a rumpled, water-pocked highland that extends all the way to Canada. The effect of ice on the topography here has been enormous. When the last ice sheet effectively blocked the natural eastward flow of many western rivers, they turned south. Their combined waters created a single great river, the Missouri, the water highway traveled by Lewis and Clark in their 1804–6 quest for an inland water route to the Pacific.

South Dakota's eastern plains once supported an almost unfathomable wealth of game—bison herds that stretched from horizon to distant horizon, huge numbers of elk and pronghorn, and sky-darkening flocks of migratory ducks, geese, and other waterfowl. Amid such abundance, Plains Indians—predominantly the Mandan, Arikara, Cheyenne, and Sioux—flourished for hundreds of years, developing complex, self-sustaining cultures. First European diseases sweeping westward in advance of settlement, then waves of settlers themselves put an end to traditional Plains Indian society. Armed resistance slowed the crush of white expansion only momentarily, and within a century the last of the tribes formally capitulated, the final spark of militant independence snuffed out on December 28, 1890, at Wounded Knee. Today tribal nations are confined to reservations that occupy about ten percent of the state's land and include some of the poorest counties in the nation.

The parched lands west of the Missouri roll away in a succession of widely spaced hills, dramatic, isolated buttes, and table-top flat plains. Dominating the state's southwest corner are the Black Hills and badlands. A forested mountain-island soaring above the treeless plain, the granite of the Hills was formed from molten magma close to a billion years ago. Today this striking landscape supports a fascinating mixture of species associated with eastern deciduous and northern coniferous forests, the treeless prairie, and Rocky Mountain ecosystems. Much is protected now by an interlocking mesh of federal and state lands—parks, forests, grasslands, and monuments. To the east stretch the badlands, South Dakota's most bizarre—and beautiful—area. A dry, sunbaked land of brightly colored pinnacles, slumps, coulees, and hoodoo peaks, this narrow strip contains one of the world's richest beds of Oligocene fossils.

In the end, as visitors invariably discover, South Dakota's profoundly different landscapes are as rich and complex as their natural histories.

THE NORTHERN TIER:
PRAIRIE POTHOLES
TO WESTERN PLAINS

When he wrote, "East is East, and West is West, and never the twain shall meet," Rudyard Kipling could have been describing South Dakota. Anyone crossing the state is struck by the profoundly dissimilar landscapes that lie on either side of the Missouri River. In the east, flat croplands—vast green and golden patchworks of corn, soybeans, oats, wheat, and hay—gently undulate away from the big river. In the west, a parched, rumpled mixed-grass prairie stretches to the horizon under flat-topped buttes and pinnacled knobs.

These landscapes unfold across the state in a series of regional ecosystems dictated by terrain, climate, and geology. East of the Missouri, South Dakota lies under a thick mantle of glacial drift, a well-drained, nutrient-rich mix of mineralized rock topped by a thick layer of organic matter—the built-up soil and root system of a 10,000-year-old prairie. Farther west, the never-glaciated land is mainly nutrient-poor clays, sands, and shales. The fossilized mud floor of an ancient sea, shale underlies the clays, sands, and silt that washed into northwest South Dakota from the slopes of the rising Rockies some 65 million years ago.

Only a thin organic layer covers these older, weathered soils, which receive little rain. Transported on westerlies robbed of moisture by the

LEFT: *Day ends spectacularly at the Sand Lake National Wildlife Refuge in northeastern South Dakota. Created in 1935 by dams in the James River, Sand Lake has become a major resting place for migratory waterfowl.*

Rockies, the weather here is good enough for sage, yucca, and such deep-rooted short- and mid-grasses as blue grama, buffalo grass, and western wheatgrass; but it is too dry for the fertile, soil-building prairie grasses and forbs of the east. Closer to the Mississippi, the climate is increasingly influenced by wetter weather moving north from the Gulf of Mexico. Eastern South Dakota receives up to 24 inches of rain a year, nearly 11 inches more than its western reaches. These disparities have produced a dramatically bifurcated state marked by rangeland in the west, farmlands in the eastern lowlands, and a mix of range and cropland in the eastern highlands.

This chapter's itinerary transects the northern tier of this natural tapestry. Beginning in the state's northeastern corner near Sisseton, it follows Route 10 across the rumpled Prairie Coteau, over the James River lowland, and up the Missouri Coteau to Mobridge and the eastern banks of the Missouri River. From Mobridge, the trip continues west on Route 12 through the vast Standing Rock Reservation to explore the state's stark northwestern corner, visiting exquisite forest-topped buttes and concluding at the sacred site of Bear Butte.

THE NORTHEAST CORNER: THE PRAIRIE COTEAU

When he recorded his first view of the imposing highland known as the Coteau des Prairies, north of Sisseton, French cartographer Joseph Nicollet permitted emotion to seep into his scientific observations: "An imposing mass," he noted in his journal on August 16, 1839, "beautiful to the eyes which have seen nothing but plains and rolling plateaus. It is the Alps of this region."

Nicollet's observation still resonates for travelers numbed by the flat terrain. Rising abruptly some 750 feet above the treeless plain, these wooded hills are hard to miss. They extend from North Dakota nearly to Nebraska, and form the eastern side of a long wedge-shaped pile of glacial debris that is high enough above the surrounding plain to be seen from space. In some places, the thick quartzite highland that once caused the ice to dump its load here lies more than 400 feet below the glacial till.

Along the scarp's northeast edge near Sisseton, the ice was forced to climb the side of the old highland, so the coteau reaches its highest point here. Taking advantage of the elevation, the **Joseph Nicollet Tower**

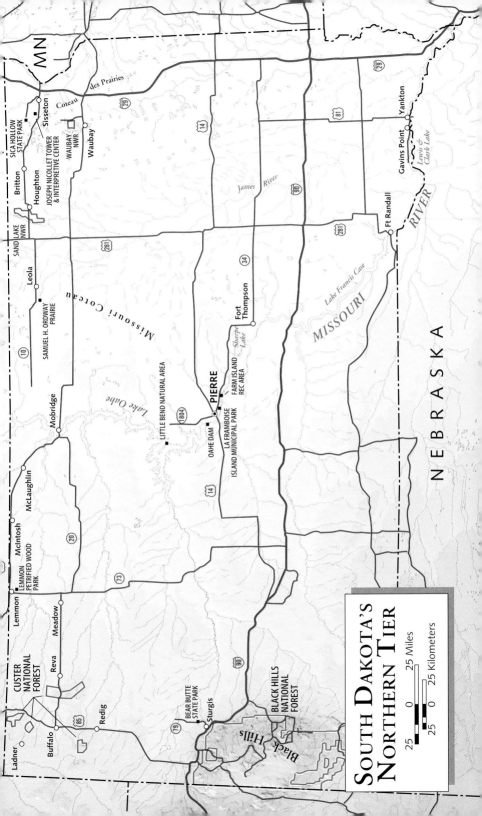

SOUTH DAKOTA'S
NORTHERN TIER

Amid grasses and wildflowers, a glacial boulder provides a hilltop perch at Sica Hollow State Park. Longfellow called these wooded draws at the edge of the Prairie Coteau "Mountains of the Prairies."

and Interpretive Center❖ perches on the highland west of town, on Route 10. The top of the tower affords a sweeping view of the coteau's pothole-laced top and scarp and the flat glacial plain below. Named for the Frenchman who mapped the region between the Missouri and Mississippi rivers in 1839, the wooden tower is adjacent to a fine interpretive center full of information about the glacial origins of the region, Joseph Nicollet's story, and the rich human history woven into these hills.

Among the distinctive aspects of this landscape are the forested ravines that crease the coteau's flank. In sharp contrast to the treeless plains below, full-size eastern deciduous woods—normally found much closer to the Mississippi—occupy these slopes. Sugar maples and basswood crowd the cooler, north-facing lower areas, bur oak forest climbs the hotter, south-facing ones, and grasslands cover the crest.

European settlers, who found similar woods all along these eastern draws, quickly turned the timber into firewood, homesteads, and towns. At least one forested coulee, however, retains a semblance of the woods that climbed the coteau's eastern flank: Sica Hollow, a particularly large wooded ravine about 15 miles northwest of Sisseton. (From Route 10, take County Route 6 north for seven miles, then head west six miles on County 12.) Now public property, **Sica Hollow State**

Park❖ is also a Native American holy place. According to centuries-old tradition, the hollow is inhabited by spirits of the dead. (Sica, pronounced *SHE-cha*, is a Dakota word for bad.) Safe by day, the place was to be avoided at night, when springs ran red with blood, and moans of departed spirits rose from the ground. On some nights, light-suffused wraiths floated among the trees in the wet bottomlands.

Although these legends, like many powerful myths, are doubtless based on firsthand observation, Sica's unusual phenomena are probably more closely connected to hydrology than to the paranormal. The ravine is riddled with seeps and calcareous fens, and much of its bottomland is bog. Because the soil is rich in iron oxide, waters do run red in places, occasionally transporting rust-stained mosses and other debris that look for all the world like bloody flesh. During spring thaws, air trapped in bog muck is released, creating a low tone similar to one produced by blowing air across the top of an open bottle. Such sounds—especially when heard at night and combined with foxfire-charged methane gas released from rotting vegetation—are enough to frighten anyone.

The hollow's moist lowlands are rife with woodland wildflowers including jack-in-the-pulpits, wood lilies, wood anemones, Solomon's seal, false Solomon's seal, touch-me-nots, and Virginia waterleaf. Red dogwoods grow here—along with ironwood, serviceberry, chokecherry, silver maple, and box elder—and wild roses, hawthorn, sumac, and big and little bluestem carpet the uplands. Among the raptors that work the ridgetop are bald and golden eagles, 8 species of hawks, and 4 species of owls; more than 150 kinds of birds, most of them eastern species, live in the lush woodlands.

PRAIRIE POTHOLES AND LOWLAND REFUGES: WAUBAY TO ORDWAY PRAIRIE

At the coteau's high northern end, the landscape is largely treeless grassland dotted with sloughs, marshes, fens, lakes, and potholes. This area forms part of South Dakota's share of the North American Prairie Pothole Region, a profusion of permanent, semipermanent, seasonal, and temporary wetlands that once stretched from northern Iowa to Alberta. The water-permeated terrain provided nesting grounds for tens of millions of migratory birds and migration refueling stops for hun-

Above: *A striking Asian import, the ring-necked pheasant is just one of nearly 250 bird species found at the Waubay National Wildlife Refuge.*

dreds of millions more. More than half of these wetlands are gone—plowed, drained, converted to cropland.

Generally permanent, the wetlands remaining on the coteau lie particularly thick across the highland's northern half. At their center is **Waubay National Wildlife Refuge❖**, a 4,650-acre federal preserve just north of the town of Waubay, which means "nesting place for birds" in the Sioux language. (County Route 1 leads north from Route 12 to the refuge entrance. Those interested in exploring more of the coteau wetlands will need a U.S. Geological Survey map to zigzag along the unnamed gravel roads from Route 10 south to the refuge.)

Some 250 species of birds have been observed at Waubay, and among the more than 100 kinds nesting there are blue-winged teal (the most abundant species on the refuge), white pelicans, cormorants, a variety of ducks, Canada geese, and 5 species of grebes. Some 39,000 acres in the surrounding six counties have been purchased specifically to provide waterfowl and shorebird habitat, and an additional 90,000 acres are protected from draining and filling by conservation agreements with landowners.

Farther west on Route 10, the highway gradually descends from the coteau to a lowland leveled by the lobe of the last glacier. West of Brit-

Left: *A stand of American basswood—whose fragrant creamy flowers attract clouds of bees—borders a rocky stream in Sica Hollow State Park.*

The Sand Lake refuge shelters millions of birds each year, including the marsh-loving pied-billed grebe (below left). The preserve is noted

ton the road crosses the flat former bed of Glacial Lake Dakota, a pool of meltwater that drained away some 10,000 years ago. About 20 miles west of Britton, on the western edge of the glacial lake, is **Sand Lake National Wildlife Refuge❖.** (Near Houghton, County Route 16 leads south from Route 10 about two and a half miles to refuge headquarters.) Encompassing more than 21,450 acres of wetlands and uplands managed for waterfowl and other wildlife, the refuge is strung along an 18-mile stretch of the James River—a natural oasis in a vast expanse of industrial agriculture. Although small dams at the south end and midsection of the refuge have created artificial lakes, the surrounding marsh and wetland habitats are a fair representation of the bygone landscape that once spread across the central lowlands.

In the spring, Sand Lake is a major staging area for snow geese bound for the arctic tundra. Winging north from the Platte River bottoms, the geese and a host of other migrating waterfowl start appearing in early to mid-March. Although the arrival date of the great flocks varies from year to year depending on temperature and weather conditions, visitors are generally assured of seeing spectacular massings of snow

for its tremendous numbers of transient snow geese (above left) and for its giant Canada geese (above right), a race once thought extinct.

geese around the last week in March. Congregating in clamoring flocks that in some years approach half a million to a million, the birds blanket the open lakes and surrounding fields like white confetti.

Besides snow geese, large populations of other species also gather here, including scaup, ring-necked ducks, ruddy ducks, pintail, redheads, shovelers, gadwalls, hooded mergansers, teal, bald eagles, numerous kinds of hawks, swans, sandhill cranes, greater white-fronted and Canada geese, pelicans—in all, more than 230 bird species. The first of these species begin to arrive in early March, with different species continuing to migrate through the refuge until mid- to late April. The refuge can be navigated by foot or car along a gravel road that follows the perimeter, and a hundred-foot tower provides a panoramic view of the surrounding area. The refuge is a key player in a larger, mostly unseen natural drama. For a few weeks each spring, a ghost landscape sometimes reappears when the bare agricultural fields become a sea of

OVERLEAF: *Maximilian's sunflowers brighten the rim of a prairie pothole at the Nature Conservancy's Samuel H. Ordway prairie preserve.*

199

LEFT: *Magenta spikes of native prairie blazing star reach above the grasses at the Ordway preserve.*

RIGHT: *Grassy swales, rolling hills, and some 400 watery potholes lace Ordway Prairie, which was home to the Cut-Head Sioux before European settlement.*

small pools. The bane of farmers, who cannot plant until they're gone, these wet spots are remnants of the old prairie wetlands that covered nearly 80 percent of these central lowlands before the advent of industrial agriculture. Dry most of the year, these temporary wetlands became veritable ponds in the spring. Because they were shallow and small, they quickly warmed, triggering an explosion of microscopic life: algae, amphipods, copopods, midge and mosquito larvae. Thus the ponds provided a protein feast for migrating waterfowl and gave dabbling ducks the seclusion needed to form pairs, nest, and breed.

Nearly a century of draining and filling have erased more than half of these lowlands, keeping fields conveniently dry for planting. In particularly wet years, however, the pools reappear like the fabled Brigadoon to play their ancient role. Although they no longer offer nesting cover (the refuge and retired cropland must suffice), these temporary wetlands provide the birds with the isolated ponds they need to form bonded pairs. Although agriculture has adversely affected them more than other types of potholes, the puddles ("pair ponds" to wildlife managers), still roll out the insect banquet. A drive through the region during a wet spring reveals vast fields blanketed in wallowing ducks—a striking reminder that humanity's relentless campaign against the natural order of things has not been entirely successful.

West of Sand Lake, as Route 10 nears the town of Leola, the land begins to rise in a series of low rolling hills. The southern end of the Missouri Coteau, the huge wetland-riddled glacial moraine left at the leading edge of the last ice sheet, this range of stepped uplands culminates at the Missouri River, some 70 miles to the west. For geographers, the uplands are the beginning, the eastern fringe, of the Great Plains. Paralleling the Missouri River and extending south to the Nebraska border, these hills assume different names in other locations. Known here

as the Leola Hills, to the south they become the Pony Hills, the Ree Heights, and the Bijou Hills.

In their sweep and aspect, the tallgrass and mixed-grass prairies that occupied these southern hills and wet swales must have been breathtaking—radiantly rolling "breakers of bluejoint" noted early twentieth-century author Hamlin Garland. Here, near Ordway, this native son and noted chronicler of the settlement period homesteaded with his family during the 1870s. Although most of the landscapes he described are long gone—the wetlands drained, the grasslands plowed—in the Leola Hills a piece of what he knew has survived.

ABOVE: *Plains Indian women made animal-shaped natal charms, enclosing a piece of the umbilical cord, for their newborn babies; this colorful snake is from about 1890.*

Some nine miles west of Leola on Route 10 (look for a kiosk on the south side of the road) is the Nature Conservancy's **Samuel H. Ordway Prairie❖,** a magnificent 7,800-acre remnant of a once truly awesome open space. Tucked away in these grassy hills, some 400 potholes ranging in size from 120 acres to small soggy spots in grassy swales can support as many as 2,000 nesting pairs of ducks in a wet year. Pintail, ruddy ducks, gadwalls, shovelers, lesser scaup, and wigeon nest here regularly, along with Wilson's phalaropes, black terns, American bitterns, and ground-nesting ferruginous hawks. Because prairie fires and grazing bison maintained the health and vigor of these grasses in the past, the preserve conducts periodic controlled burns and maintains a small herd of 125 bison. More than 300 plant species flourish here, and the prairie is in bloom most of the growing season. Grasses—western wheatgrass, big and little bluestem, switchgrass, blue grama—and such wildflowers as wild roses, purple coneflowers, pasqueflowers, and meadow anemones punctuate the uplands. Sedges and cordgrass border the swales, and cattails and bulrushes grow in wetter areas and standing water. Self-guided hiking tours of varying length extend throughout this splendid undulating expanse.

ALONG THE GREAT MISSOURI

West of Ordway Prairie, the rolling hills of the Missouri Coteau continue to rise until they reach the **Missouri River**—or more accurately, what's left of it. In fact, very little of the legendary river of Lewis and Clark flows unimpeded through South Dakota. Dams at Pierre, Fort Thompson, Fort Randall, and Gavins Point, south of Yankton, have turned all but 100 miles of the river in the state into a series of reservoirs—Lakes Oahe, Sharpe, Francis Case, and Lewis and Clark. As recently as 200 years ago, the valley of the big, winding Missouri and its bottomlands and lower breaks (the woody draws that ran up its flanks) constituted a unique, complex ecosystem, a world rich in wildlife. In 1804 Meriwether Lewis and William Clark noted in their journals the huge herds of pronghorn, elk, and bison here and the correspondingly large numbers of wolves and coyotes that attended them. (South Dakota is still known as the Coyote State.) Both mule and white-tailed deer wandered the region, as did black bears, grizzlies, and bighorn sheep.

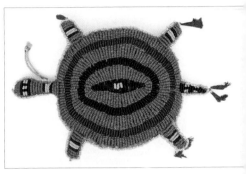

ABOVE: *A natal charm such as this 1885 beaded turtle served first as a cradle toy; it was then worn around the neck and kept forever as an amulet to ensure its owner a long life.*

Along the river and its channels, marshes and sloughs supported many waterfowl and shorebirds: whooping and sandhill cranes, plover, curlews, wigeon, pintail, scaup, ringnecks, swans, and snow geese. Turkeys, warblers, woodpeckers, flycatchers, and an abundance of songbirds populated the big cottonwood forests that occurred sporadically along the lower terraces and on the river's juniper, cottonwood, and willow-thicket sandbar and gravel islands. Great flocks of sharp-tailed grouse worked along the river's edges. Lewis and Clark found people here too. Scattered along the lower terraces stood the clustered earthen lodges of the Arikara and Mandan, their small gardens of squash, beans, corn, and tobacco spread on the floodplain below.

Through it all wound the grand coffee-and-cream–colored Missouri (the Dakota word for muddy), a watery expanse "too thin to plow, and too thick to drink" according to local adage. Always moving, shifting its bed, opening new channels and erasing old ones, the river ran under banks of loamy sand and soft shales. As it cut a corner here and rounded off a bend there, the Missouri constantly recarved its trench. Deeply undercut sand banks fell crashing into the river, bringing with them trees, prairie, and anything else living on top. Channels were frequently choked with fallen timber, trees whose roots and branches clawed the current just out of sight, inches below the water's surface. A nightmare for navigators, the Missouri provided rich habitat for sauger, pike, walleye and other perch, paddlefish, buffalo fish, sheepshead, and sturgeon.

By the close of the nineteenth century, the grizzlies, elk, wolves, bison, pronghorn, and whooping cranes had been eradicated as settlement closed the book on the midcontinental frontier. Native Americans were relegated to the sprawling, devastatingly poor reservations that still cover about ten percent of South Dakota. Between 1953 and 1964, water behind four huge earthen dams inundated most of the remaining Missouri River valley—the snags, the sandbars, the wooded islands, the floodplain forests, the lower terraces, the old Indian village sites—leaving only the upper slopes of the old valley and the upper reaches of the river's woody breaks. Now a string of game management areas and boat access points running along the Missouri's eastern bank from Mobridge to I-90 and then on both sides of the river to the Nebraska border, these places—**Whitlocks Bay, Sutton Bay, Mail Shack Creek, Peoria Flats,** among others—are a pheasant-hunter's paradise.

Of particular note is the **Little Bend Natural Area✦,** a bit of wild Missouri River upland at the head of a dramatic promontory extending into Lake Oahe some 38 miles north of Pierre. (The site is west of Route 1804; look for a sign and gravel road heading west.) Once a sharp turn in the river that nearly doubled back on itself, Little Bend is now a rugged, steep peninsula. Falling away sharply on either side, the promontory's dark shale and clay flanks are cut by deep wooded coulees that become open grasslands on top. A single dirt road traverses the peninsula, and the high natural area is about a mile's walk from the flat, shimmering waters of the lake. Wildflowers abound, among them American vetch, prairie coneflower, broom snakeweed, and western wallflower. Silver sage and western wheatgrass grow on the upland, and yucca dots the drier slopes.

Near Pierre, a few miles below the Oahe Dam, two wooded islands—La Framboise and Farm—lie in a remnant stretch of the old Missouri, a narrow reach that would probably be recognizable to Lewis and Clark. Just south of the city, **La Framboise Island Natural Area**❖ is a wooded sandbar representative of the many smaller islands that once lay scattered up and down the river's channel. From Steamboat Park, follow the river to the causeway leading to the island. Today a U.S. Army Corps of Engineers natural area, La Framboise is a good birding spot; it is dominated by a remnant stand of large cottonwoods, along with green ashes and box elders, and features a small prairie in its interior. Visitors can see both eastern and western bird species from the marked trails.

Farm Island State Recreational Area❖ is centered on another wooded island some two miles east of Pierre off Route 34. Here, cottonwoods are declining and dryland species and exotics are on the rise. Near this 1,800-acre site, members of the Lewis and Clark expedition beached their pirogues to retrieve elk shot by expedition hunters.

Farm Island is a birding hot spot and a "hybrid zone" for a number of closely related avian species whose eastern and western ranges overlap: red- and yellow-shafted flickers, Bullock's and Baltimore orioles, western and eastern races of rufous-sided towhees. Routinely seen here are yellow-headed blackbirds, black-billed cuckoos, Virginia rail, and many species of waterfowl, shorebirds, wood warblers, hawks, turkeys, magpies, and other species common to western and eastern regions. The visitor center is on the mainland, and a 1.5-mile self-guided nature trail listed on the National Registry of Recreation Hiking Trails traverses the island.

The Northwest: Prairies, Fossils, and Buttes

West of the Missouri the mid- and short-grass prairie begins. On windswept summer days, this pitching gray-green sea is transformed into a moving mosaic of myriad shades and hues. In early morning, slanting sunlight catches the mist in the coulees, enveloping the landscape in an otherworldly beauty. Blue grama, little bluestem, buffalo grass, and west-

---

Overleaf: *Near Reva Gap, the Castles of Slim Buttes rise like the parapets and turrets of some medieval fortress. In these wooded draws the Sioux took refuge from U.S. troops during the 1876 Battle of Slim Buttes.*

ern wheatgrass blanket the parched clay and shaley soils. Prickly pear and yucca grow on the hotter slopes, while sage, buckbrush, and rabbitbrush gather in the draws. A land of pronghorn, rattlesnakes, and towering solitary buttes, it seems a world away from the country east of the river.

Time is writ large on this landscape. Geological events of the past have strongly affected the look of the land and the life it now supports, but that ancient natural history is revealed today only in fragments—on the banded faces of solitary buttes, in the cutbanks above the rivers that carve their way to the Missouri, in the scattered fossils that rains wash from the sides of countless dry coulees.

Route 12 from Mobridge to Lemmon traverses the remote grasslands of the sparsely populated Standing Rock Reservation and cuts across the fossil residue of a number of prehistoric landscapes. West of Mobridge the highway passes over shale deposited some 75 million years ago, when South Dakota rested on the bottom of a shallow Cretaceous sea. By McLaughlin, shales have been replaced by sandstones deposited some 5 to 10 million years later in shallow shoreline waters. Nearing McIntosh, the terrain is chiefly sandstone from wide rivers negotiating a hot, humid lowland. The final stage is a mishmash of sandstones, siltstones, sand, and clays formed about 63 million years ago in a vast steamy landscape of lakes, swamps, and winding, sluggish rivers. Approaches to Lemmon from the west, east, or south pass through this same sequence of ever-younger surface rocks. Arcing south across northwestern South Dakota, all lie at or within the southern rim of the Williston Basin, a 200,000-square-mile depression in the continental crust that was for millions of years a catchment for sea sediments as well as silts and sands carried off the flanks of the rising Rocky Mountains. Over the ages, younger layers of debris piled over older ones.

Because different beds preserve different kinds of prehistoric life, South Dakota is one of the world's great fossil centers. One bed south of Lemmon, between the Grand and Moreau rivers, contains some of the most notorious megafauna of the late Cretaceous—tyrannosaurs, triceratops, hadrosaurs, and a host of others.

Lemmon lies in a region that has yielded a prolific quantity of petrified wood, the fossilized remnants of a great redwood forest that stood here some 60 million years ago. Shards of petrified wood can be found scattered throughout the low hills around the town, along with the fossil prints of dinosaurs, grasses, and leaves impressed in area sandstones. Worth a stop, the city's **Lemmon Petrified Wood Park❖** is a fantasyland of multicolored statuary constructed entirely of petrified wood collected from the surrounding countryside and assembled in whimsical castles, spires, and pyramids. Originating as a public project during the Great Depression, the park displays some truly magnificent specimens.

Southwest of Lemmon (43 miles west of Meadow on Route 20), a collection of forest-topped buttes rise like pharaonic ruins on the treeless plain, the chalky creams and whites and pastel yellows and browns of their banded buttresses, scarps, and parapets standing out

212

The Northwest: Prairies, Fossils, and Buttes

LEFT: *The white cliff faces of the Castles at Slim Buttes turn tawny in the setting sun. Topped by hard sandstones, these ancient sedimentary formations have yielded the fossil remains of a host of prehistoric life.*

in sharp contrast to the deep green of the ponderosa pine forest covering them. Curiously, some 10 million years younger than any other butte or upland in this quarter of the state, the buttes are soft sedimentary rocks capped by hard channel sandstone, once the sandy bottoms of wide Oligocene rivers. The rocky layers in these sedimentary formations range in age from the volcanic ash at the top, blown here from the west some 26 million years ago, to the 65-million-year-old shales and sandstones at the bottom.

Lying just west of Reva, the largest of these promontories is **Slim Buttes❖,** site of a post–Little Bighorn skirmish between the U.S. Army and a band of Oglala Sioux. In September 1876, General George Crook stumbled on a village of Oglala and Minneconjou at the foot of these buttes. Although most of the Sioux escaped, their leader, American Horse, 3 warriors, and about 15 women and children holed up in a cave in one of the coulees. Passing into history as the Battle of Slim Buttes, the daylong firefight ended with the surrender of the Oglala and the death of American Horse, one of his warriors, and an undetermined number of women and children.

An L-shaped highland running some 20 miles north and south, Slim Buttes lives up to its name because it is never more than five miles wide. The west side is sheer, its castlelike scarp plunging several hundred feet to the plain. On the east a series of deeply dissected arroyos and ridges ascend to a steeply rolling pine savanna. On the top the forested highlands are often parklike. Stands of pines punctuate the grassland and disappear down coulees under high cream-colored bluffs. Little patches of pure prairie skirt the western scarp, and along the lower slopes, pine forest gives way to mixed woodland of green ash and chokecherry.

Bobcat and wild turkeys wander the woodlands, while mule deer, pronghorn, sharp-tailed grouse, and coyotes occupy the highlands.

Left: *Pine cone seeds from the ponderosas that populate the far-flung Custer National Forest sustain both squirrels and nuthatches.*

Right: *The slanting light of early evening transforms the sedimentary rock at North Cave Hills into a natural mosaic resembling rococo filigree.*

Eagle-catching sites and evidence of Indian burial grounds can be found in some of the arroyos. Also rich in fossils, these hills hold the petrified remains of many prehistoric creatures—small horses, pigs, tapirs, saber-toothed cats, turtles, assorted shrews, moles, and a hippolike Metamynodon. The numerous trails meandering through the buttes, which are managed by the **Custer National Forest❖**, provide stunning vistas and access to such special places as the Castles, pretty Reva Valley, and Eagles Nest Canyon. Drive-in primitive camping at Reva Gap campground south of Route 20 makes a good base for exploring the surrounding area.

Some 20 miles west of Slim Buttes (take the JB Road) and four or five miles west of Route 85 on Mackey Road is a string of mini-badlands known as the **Jump-offs.** North of the road extensive erosion has caused the land to fall away, creating a wild jumble of deeply cleft wooded coulees, intricately gullied scarps, and clay slumps that drop in tiers to the flat plain far below. Travelers experience this starkly beautiful countryside in a fine looping drive that begins on Mackey Road heading west to Forest Road 897 and then curving north to Route 20 and the town of Buffalo.

About 20 miles northwest of Slim Buttes and 10 miles north of the town of Buffalo, two smaller buttes, **North** and **South Cave Hills❖,** are just as beautiful, albeit not so dramatic, as their better-known cousins to the south. Parklike ponderosa pine and savanna cloak the steep uplands in this section of the Custer National Forest. Numerous petroglyphs have been etched and pecked into rock faces in the deep draws and wooded coulees that dissect the flanks of North Cave Hills. To explore smaller and less accessible forest-topped highlands in this region, a Forest Service map (available from the Sioux Ranger office in

RIGHT: *Bear Butte, a plug of hardened magma looming above the short-grass prairie just north of the Black Hills, is not only a premier state park but also a sacred place for both the Cheyenne and Lakota peoples.*

Camp Crook or from forest headquarters in Billings, Montana) is a necessity.

Farther south on Route 85, beyond Redig, the highway crosses a vast shaley grass and sage plain. This is Butte County, named for the massive prominences that rise from the level land like a scattered convoy of ships on a gray-green sea. Bearing names like Two Top, Deers Ear, Owl, Eagle, Antelope, Haystack, Mud, Geographical Center of the Nation (which it is not), and Castle Rock, these buttes have long figured prominently in Native American history and culture as places to catch eagles, to enshrine the dead, to experience visions, to take shelter. **Crow Butte,** just west of Route 85 a couple of miles south of Redig, is a good example. In the summer of 1822, a war party of Lakota jumped a Crow camp on the banks of Sand Creek, a few miles north of the butte. A number of Crow warriors escaped, taking refuge on the butte. The Lakota surrounded them and settled down to wait, holding the Crow hostage until they died of thirst.

About 60 miles south of Crow Butte and 10 miles north of Sturgis on Route 79, a massive body of rock called **Bear Butte** is a sacred site to Native Americans. Rising to 4,426 feet, the butte is actually a laccolith, a huge block of once molten magma that hardened beneath the earth's surface and forced the overlying rock to be uplifted. The combination of geologic forces that caused this cone of rock—and the Black Hills a few miles farther south—to rise is still a mystery; but

those forces are of little concern to the Cheyenne and Lakota, who
have for centuries considered the butte holy. The Lakota named it
Mato Paha, or sleeping bear. The Cheyenne call it Noah' wus, the
place where Maheo, the creator, gave their cultural hero Sweet Medicine four sacred arrows that let him convey the creator's supernatural
life to his people. Both Lakota and Cheyenne make annual pilgrim-
ages to sacred places on the mountain. Bear Butte is also a popular
climb for families, and hiking trails lead to the top through juniper and
ponderosa pine savanna. **Bear Butte State Park**❖ maintains a visitor
center as well as year-round camping and recreational facilities.

217

THE SOUTHERN TIER:
BLACK HILLS
AND BADLANDS

To the Lakota, they were Paha Sapa, the hills that are black—
a holy place. To the gold seekers who ultimately wrested
them from the Native Americans, they were a land of wealth
and opportunity. To the hordes of tourists who trek to them
today, they are among the most spectacular natural wonders in the
country. The Black Hills are indeed unique.

Covering nearly 6,000 square miles, they rise unexpectedly like an
elliptical blister above the surrounding plain—a virtual mini–mountain
range some 120 miles north to south and 50 miles across at midsection.
In this southwest corner of the state, the persistent hand of water and
wind have sculpted a staggeringly beautiful landscape of high granite
ridges and deep tree-shaded gorges. The skyline—a cavalcade of clustered pinnacles, hoodoo peaks, and curiously shaped knobs—continu-
ally amazes. Underground, the scenery is no less spectacular because
the ancient limestone here has yielded some of the largest—and most
intricately embellished—caverns in the world.

Collectively, the Black Hills are the eroded remnants of what geologists call a mountainous upthrust, a bubble of magma that began push-
ing up through the earth's crust close to a billion years ago—about 90
million years before the birth of the Rockies. Experts speculate that as
sediments settled to the bottom of a huge inland sea, the accumulated

---

LEFT: *A summer shower softens the pastel-colored surfaces of the sedi-*
ments in the Yellow Mounds area of Badlands National Park, where
water and erosion have created a striking and otherworldly landscape.

---

weight created enough pressure to force the magma beneath the seafloor to expand upward. This cooled and crystallized into granite, which was later exposed by erosion. Younger rocks were deposited above the granite, and the entire Black Hills area was lifted along faults at the same time the Rocky Mountains formed. Under intense heat and pressure, the overlying sediments were bent, folded, and cooked into some of the varicolored rocks in the Hills today. The process took several hundred million years, including a succession of uplifts, periods of erosion, sea inundations, and the final uplift about a million years ago. Since then, erosion on a massive scale, by wind and especially water, has been ceaselessly at work.

This complex geologic history is illustrated in the four dramatically distinct topographical features that comprise the Hills and the badlands immediately to the east. Circling the central uplift, the first is a hogback ridge that rises some 3,800 to 4,900 feet above the plain. Topped by ponderosa pine, this hard sandstone ridge is nearly continuous, broken only where major streams coursing off the Hills have managed to erode their way through. Between the ridge and the uplift, the second feature, a narrow grassy valley, rings the base of the uplift. Now formally named the Red Valley, this circular grassland was called the racetrack by the Lakota and Cheyenne, to whom the Hills were sacred.

Lining the inside of the racetrack, the third feature is a band of foothills. Crowding the base of the massif to the north, in the south they spread out into a broad tableland known as the Minnekahta Plains. Inside the foothills rises the fourth element, the central mass of the Black Hills, a flat-topped plateau of sedimentary material. Chiefly limestone mixed with sandstones and shale, it is the accumulated floors of countless seas. Atop this base, at about 5,000 feet, stands the spectacularly eroded core of the Hills: the granitic batholith rising out of the baked and transformed sedimentary material—quartzites, slates, and schists.

The prolonged birth of the Black Hills also had a dramatic effect on the lands to the east. Repeated episodes of deposition, uplift, and erosion sent massive amounts of clay and sand coursing off the uplift and across the plain below. (In the final series of uplifts alone, an estimated 6,500 feet of sediment washed away.) Today these mudstones, claystones, and siltstones make up a topography known as the badlands. In a 90-mile trench east across the Dakota grasslands, these for-

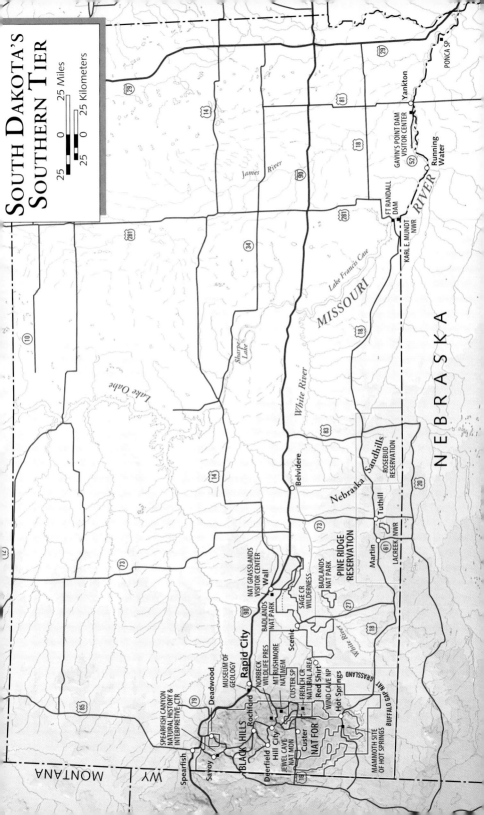

SOUTH DAKOTA'S SOUTHERN TIER

25   0   25 Miles
25   0   25 Kilometers

MONTANA

WY

MONTANA

NEBRASKA

MISSOURI

RIVER

Lake Oahe

Sharpe Lake

James River

Lake Francis Case

White River

Nebraska Sandhills

ROSEBUD RESERVATION

PINE RIDGE RESERVATION

BADLANDS NAT PARK

NAT GRASSLANDS VISITOR CENTER

Wall

SAGE CR WILDERNESS

Scenic

BADLANDS NAT PARK

Belvidere

Yankton

GAVIN'S POINT DAM VISITOR CENTER

Running Water

FT RANDALL DAM

KARLE MUNDT NWR

PONCA SP

Tuthill

Martin

LACREEK NWR

Rapid City

Deadwood

MUSEUM OF GEOLOGY

SPEARFISH CANYON NATURAL HISTORY & INTERPRETIVE CTR

Spearfish

Savoy

BLACK HILLS

Rochford

Deerfield

Hill City

JEWEL CAVE NAT MON

Custer

NAT FOR

NORBECK WILDLIFE PRES

MT RUSHMORE NAT MEM

CUSTER SP

FRENCH CR NATURAL AREA

Red Shirt

WIND CAVE NP

Hot Springs

NAT GRASSLAND

BUFFALO GAP

MAMMOTH SITE OF HOT SPRINGS

LEFT: *The clear, cold waters of a highland stream tumble out of a side canyon down into Spearfish Creek at the northern end of the Black Hills.*
RIGHT: *Found throughout the forests of the Black Hills, the sharp-shinned hawk preys on smaller birds, often ambushing them from a hidden perch.*

mations are a virtual geologic fantasyland of intricately fluted pinnacles, brightly banded scarps—golds, rusts, browns, mauves, and silver grays that shimmer in the sun—and chalk-faced tablelands.

Exploring this rugged, starkly beautiful region should not be undertaken lightly. Because many roads are unpaved and unmarked, detailed topographical maps—available from the National Park Service, the Forest Service, and at many individual sites—are essential. Four-wheel drive is often necessary, and many areas, particularly in the badlands, are impassable when wet. Travelers should never set out without substantial supplies, especially of water and fuel.

Beginning at the town of Spearfish, north of the uplift, this chapter proceeds south through a picturesque gorge onto the limestone plateau. From there it swings southwest into the granitic core of the Black Hills, then east and south through Custer State Park and Wind Cave National Park to the Mammoth Site west of Hot Springs. Moving eastward, the itinerary winds south through both units of Badlands National Park and across the southern tier of the state to the Missouri River.

BLACK HILLS NATIONAL FOREST

From I-90 near the Wyoming border, one of the loveliest routes into **Black Hills National Forest❖** is up **Spearfish Canyon❖,** a deep, twisting gorge that Spearfish Creek has cut into the surrounding limestone plateau. Armed with a U.S. Forest Service map, begin in the town of Spearfish and head south on Route 14A, a national forest scenic byway. Hugging the creek, the blacktop gradually ascends the canyon skirting sheer limestone cliffs. A deciduous forest of oaks, ashes, willows, and aspens shades the lower gorge but gives way to dark stands of thick ponderosa pines farther up the canyon walls.

Near Savoy, Little Spearfish Creek tumbles out of the highlands from the west and plunges over **Roughlock Falls** into the larger stream below. (The falls are a short hike south of the junction of Forest Road 222 and Route 14A.) This area is one of the few in the Black Hills where American dippers work the fast-moving streams. Running into the swift current, these small, plump gray birds literally walk under crashing mountain waters to feed along the stream bottom. Film buffs take note: Unspoiled Little Spearfish Canyon was the setting for the final winter scene from Kevin Costner's epic film *Dances with Wolves.*

ABOVE: *Red trillium thrives in the forests of the Black Hills, well west of its normal range.*

RIGHT: *In lower Spearfish Canyon, a vibrant cottonwood dressed for autumn signals the imminent arrival of winter.*

The **Spearfish Canyon Natural History and Cultural Center**❖ at the nearby Latchstring Village resort complex is well worth a visit. Along with the affiliated Interpretive Nature Theater, the center offers a compelling multimedia exhibition on the natural history of the region. Displays chronicle gold mining in the Hills from the initial pan-and-shovel gold rush triggered by George Armstrong Custer's 1874 exploratory expedition to the introduction of the big stamp-mill ore processors of the 1940s.

South of Cheyenne Crossing (an 1880s stop on the stage route between Deadwood and Cheyenne), Route 85 continues up Spearfish Canyon and the limestone plateau. As the road climbs and nears the top, the land on either side opens up and dark pine changes to aspen forest—a spectacular sight when fall paints the landscape orange and gold. Here white-tailed and mule deer, wild turkeys, and elk wander the woodlands, and eagles and hawks ride the warm thermals that rise from the canyon. At O'Neil Pass, a gravel road entering from the left (Forest Road 231) proceeds southeast across the top of the plateau into the rugged heart of the Black Hills. Along the way, aspen yields

to savanna and ponderosa pine, and then to a white spruce forest as the road begins to descend into the narrow, winding, and surpassingly lovely **Black Fox Canyon.** Thick-trunked spruce, often draped with the wispy tangles of Usnea moss called old-man's beard close in over the road. In this primeval-looking forest—as close to virgin timber as any woods in the Black Hills—minimally maintained tracks that make good hiking and mountain-biking routes disappear into the forest from the main road along this stretch. South of the campground on 231, the forest becomes a typical Black Hills mixture: spruce on the cooler north-facing slopes, pine on the hotter south-facing ones. Four miles south of Rochford as County Route 306 heads toward Deerfield, the pines suddenly give way to a rolling montane grassland.

Reynolds Prairie❖, about 15 square miles, is the largest of several naturally occurring grasslands in these wooded highlands. Why the land is unforested here remains a mystery. South of Reynolds Prairie, County Route 306/17 intersects Forest Road 110. To the right, 110 ascends Castle Creek Valley to the west. More than a century ago, this well-grazed pastureland was a vivid sea of grass and wildflowers growing in astonishing profusion. Upon entering the valley on his famous 1874 expedition through the Black Hills, George Armstrong Custer was so overcome by the sight that he called the place **Floral Valley.** Describing his encounter in his official report, Custer wrote: "Every step of our march that day was amid flowers of the most exquisite colors and perfume.... It was a strange sight to glance back at the advancing columns of cavalry and behold the men with beautiful bouquets in their hands, while the headgear of the horses was decorated with wreaths of flowers fit to Crown a Queen of May." At one stop, 17 identifiable floral "varieties" were collected within a 20-foot area. Flowers seen there today include golden pea, coneflower, sunflower, iris, fleabane, yarrow, wood lily, oxeye daisy, shooting star, rose, verbena, lupine, penstemon, and prairie smoke. In this valley, not far from the junction of Forest Road 110 and Route 17, the troop's photographer snapped a picture of the expedition camp that became one of early photography's most famous images (a small sign marks the site).

Route 17 leads southeast into the exposed granitic core of the Black Hills and some of the most scenic country in the state. **Mount Rushmore National Memorial❖** (east of Hill City on Route 244) is an amazing testament to the skill of sculptor Gutzon Borglum, who carved and blasted the visages of four American presidents into the smooth-grained face of the 5,725-foot mountain. The enormous rock edifice is an eroded wall of granite that the Lakota people still hold sacred. Mountain goats clamber among the moss- and lichen-covered ridges above the timberline. Not native to South Dakota, they were introduced here, and in the Harney Peak and Needles areas, in 1924.

CUSTER STATE PARK

Much of this incomparable country lies within an assemblage of federal and state holdings; the largest segment is 73,000-acre **Custer State Park❖,** south of Hill City on Route 87. Situated in the southeast corner of the Black Hills, the park spans not only the granitic heart of the uplift, but a portion of the limestone plateau and surrounding foothills as well. Encompassing pine and spruce forests on the uplands, rolling mid- and short-grass prairie below, and hardwood forests on the lower slopes and in the coulees, the park offers an unusually rich assortment of habitats that sustain a wealth of wildlife.

The **Sylvan Lake** area in the northeast arm of the park is a trailhead center for a number of particularly scenic hikes and rambles. Beginning at Sylvan Lake Dam, the fairly strenuous 3.5-mile hike through **Sunday Gulch** traverses some of the most diverse terrain in the park: deep canyons with immense boulders and soaring granite walls, wildflower-splashed meadows, mixed forests of pine, spruce, and hardwoods. After descending the gulch, visitors enter the deeply eroded granite of the uplift and a remnant of the cooked and transformed sedimentary rock—quartzites, slates, and schists—that lay atop it when the granite was a rising molten bubble of magma. Much of the drama of this landscape results from the amazing ways that different types of rocks have weathered and eroded. Although granite is hard and fairly resistant to erosion, the softer sedimentary rocks weather at variable rates. Together, under the relentless hand of water and wind, these ancient strata have been transformed into an astonishing landscape of

---

OVERLEAF: *From a vantage point atop Little Devils Tower in Custer State Park, the jagged peaks of the Cathedral Spires rise up like the serrated teeth of a giant saw over the ancient granite core of the Black Hills.*

ABOVE: *A protected and now-prolific bison herd races across the short-grass prairie in Custer State Park. Standing six feet tall at the shoulder,*

impossibly sharp ridges, plummeting gorges, soaring pinnacles, phantasmagoric knobs, and magical peaks.

Excellent trails beginning in Custer's northern arm lead to **Harney Peak,** a 7,242-foot granite knob in the heart of the Harney Range that is the highest point in the United States east of the Rockies. One trail winds through a group of extraordinary granite pinnacles known as the **Cathedral Spires** and a small stand of limber pine, an uncommon species in these parts. Some of these pines are more than two centuries old, and botanists wonder whether they are remnants of a once-larger forest.

A second hiking route to Harney Peak is via **Little Devils Tower,** a granite knob reminiscent of Wyoming's Devils Tower, the gigantic volcanic monolith just to the west across the state line. The trail at Little Devils Tower (six miles round-trip) is a fine, if vigorous, family hike, and the view from the top makes the effort worthwhile.

Harney Peak and most of the Harney Range are within the 9,824-acre **Black Elk Wilderness❖,** which lies in turn within the **Norbeck Wildlife Preserve❖.** Its 35,000 acres support a rugged landscape of soaring granite peaks that rise above pine-forested canyons and steep, round-shouldered hills, deep valleys, and creek-filled coulees. In the Sylvan Lake and Needles area alone, some 300 granite spires pierce the sky, offering climbs ranging from simple boulder scrambles to 300-foot roped ascents. The preserve is laced with numerous trails—60

bulls live apart from cows and calves except during breeding season and, despite their two-ton bulk, can manage speeds of up to 32 mph.

miles are marked and mapped—that lead to spectacular vistas and provide many opportunities to encounter a wide assortment of wildlife. The area abounds with white-tailed deer, elk, bald and golden eagles, numerous songbirds from both eastern and western provinces, wild turkeys, beavers, porcupines, mountain goats, and seldom seen mountain lions. Comprehensive maps to the area can be purchased near the Sylvan Lake entrance at the park's visitor center, a Civilian Conservation Corps–built structure on the *National Register of Historic Buildings* that houses a small natural-history museum and bookstore.

Two particularly scenic roads guide visitors into the greater body of Custer State Park. The **Needles Highway** (Route 87) runs southeast from the Sylvan Lake area, entering the park at its northwest corner. **Iron Mountain Road** (Route 16A) runs southeast from Mount Rushmore, twisting and turning through a landscape of spires and pinnacles, curlicue bridges, and narrow tunnels constructed to frame the Rushmore faces.

Within the park's large southern unit, several more hiking paths traverse meadows, streams, coniferous and deciduous forests, and high plains. One of the more popular trails is **Lover's Leap,** a bracing hike that winds through ponderosa pine, skirts a high ridge, and then curls down to picturesque Galena Creek. The four-mile looping hike offers stunning views of Mount Coolidge, Cathedral Peak, and Cathedral

Winding along the high ridges of Custer State Park, the Needles Highway bisects ponderosa-pine and aspen forest (right) and affords a glimpse of a shaggy mountain goat (left), whose hooves are particularly suited to the steep, rocky topography of the Black Hills.

Spires. A wilder hike along unmarked trails takes in the 2,200-acre **French Creek Natural Area❖.** This 12-mile one-way trek meanders through a mixed forest of pine and hardwoods along the narrow granite and limestone gorge of French Creek, reputedly a fine trout stream. Dotted with boulders, this rugged canyon is good birding country that also supports bighorn sheep. The sheep, actually indigenous to the Rockies, were introduced here sometime after the native bighorn, a distinct subspecies, were extirpated.

The park's **Prairie Trail** offers an entirely different experience. One of four self-guided interpretative trails, this 3.5-mile looping trek leads through rolling mid- and short-grass prairie and affords splendid panoramic views of the surrounding Black Hills. The time to follow its undulating contours is June and July, when wildflowers such as scarlet globemallows, prairie coneflowers, dame's rocket, black-eyed susans, goldenrods, bluebells, and evening primroses are in bloom. The park's southern unit can also be toured by car on the 18-mile Wildlife Loop Road, which circles through lovely rolling hills, wooded valleys, and narrow streams. Along the way, open rangelands provide a splendid opportunity to observe herds of grazing elk and bison, graceful white-tailed deer feeding at dawn and dusk, and bustling towns of prairie dogs.

Caves, Carvings, and Hot Springs

One of the most astonishing—and exquisite—sections of the Black Hills is underground: Of the 72 known calcite crystal caves in the world, 68 are found here. The constituent material of much of this ter-

---

OVERLEAF: *In the western reaches of Wind Cave National Park, patches of sunlight dramatize the gathering clouds of a summer storm and highlight the park's green wooded ridges and golden prairie grasses.*

ABOVE: *A welcome harbinger of spring, the delicate lavender pasqueflower blooms early and is the state flower.*
RIGHT: *Great yellow swaths of western wallflowers carpet the short-grass prairie at Wind Cave National Park.*
BELOW: *The purple flowers of the western spiderwort are a late-summer delight.*

rain is limestone, which dissolves when subjected to weak carbonic or sulfuric acid. Acidic water seeping into cracks in the uplifted limestone from both above, in the form of rain, snowmelt, and streams, and below, from a subterranean water table, has over millennia literally eaten away the underlying rock, creating a vast network of channels and caverns deep within the plateau interior. As a consequence, the Hills, particularly along their eastern side, are riddled with caves and underground passageways.

Of the nine major caves in the Black Hills, two incomparably beautiful and complex ones rank among the world's premier caverns. In the southern portion of **Wind Cave National Park❖**, which is adjacent to Custer State Park's southern perimeter, **Wind Cave** is the seventh-longest limestone cavern in the world. Visitors can stroll some of the cave's more than 77 mapped miles only on guided tours, which range from lighted paved routes to a spelunker special where participants must climb and crawl. A historical version is conducted entirely by candlelight. All the tours include close-ups of the amazing underground formations: honeycombed boxwork, tangled helictite bushes, frostwork, and popcorn.

Situated in the foothills of the limestone plateau, the park encompasses about 28,000 acres of rolling grasslands and wooded hills. A good overview can be had from **Rankin Ridge,** on the west side of the park. Stretching to the horizon are magnificent vistas of rugged ridgelines, wooded hills, and sweeping grasslands to the north, east, and south. Visible to the east is Buffalo Gap, the famous break in the hogback ridge through which migrating bison once poured. On a clear day, beyond the hogback, even the badlands can

ABOVE: *Inside a facility at the Mammoth Site of Hot Springs, a worker at the Black Hills paleontological dig patiently clears away the layers of soft clay that have entombed a mammoth for more than 25,000 years.*

be discerned. The park now supports a healthy number of bison; today's managed herd of 350 began with 13 animals donated by the Bronx Zoo in 1913.

Some 13 miles west of the town of Custer on Route 16 lies the other major cavern in the Black Hills, the focus of **Jewel Cave National Monument❖.** Containing more than 100 miles of known passages and an estimated 1,000 more miles still unexplored, Jewel Cave is the world's fourth-longest cavern. It features a profusion of rare underground delights: glittering crystals ranging from translucent white to yellow and red; pointed, many-sided nailhead spar crystals; needlelike argonite frostwork; gypsum beards; and the tiny silver bubbles known as hydromagnesite balloons. Rare red scintillate can be seen here, as well as spectacular ribbon draperies, iron oxide–stained sheets of calcium carbonate. Tours accommodate the ambitions of casual walk-in visitors as well as spelunkers.

Some five miles north of Custer on Route 16 lies Thunderhead Mountain, site of the monumental **Crazy Horse Memorial❖.** Begun by the late Korczak Ziolkowski in 1947, this 563-foot granite rendition of the Oglala warrior has become a Native American counterpoint to Mount Rushmore. Although only a fraction of the huge project has been completed, the Ziolkowski family and their nonprofit foundation have expanded the project to include a visitor center and Native American museum with displays representing 80 North American tribes.

In the extreme southeast corner of the Hills, about one mile west of Hot Springs on Truck Route 18, is the **Mammoth Site of Hot Springs❖,** an enclosed paleontological excavation of an ancient sinkhole. About 26,000 years ago, a water-carved cavity in the limestone bedrock here collapsed—along with the weak shale above it—producing a steep pit. Water welling up from artesian springs quickly filled the bottom, creating a seemingly simple, albeit steep-sided, water hole. In fact, the pool became a death trap for thirsty animals because seeps under the shale made the steep slopes too slick for them to climb out. Over the course of 300 to 700 years, many animals died in the sinkhole, as did the scavengers and predators who came to feast on the dying and dead.

Excavators have now unearthed mammoths—a type of hairy prehistoric elephant—as well as timber wolves, coyotes, a camel, a peccary, extinct pronghorn, voles, jackrabbits, cottontail rabbits, ground squirrels, mink, mice, wood rats, kangaroo rats, fish, clams, and snails. At least one giant short-faced bear, a creature of immense size, was found here; some ten feet long and three feet taller than a modern grizzly at the shoulder, it probably weighed about 1,400 pounds. All became entombed in the shale and sand that kept washing into the pit. In time, the underground water dried up and the compacted layers of reworked shale and sand hardened, encasing the skeletal remains. A mammoth tusk uncovered in 1974 by a bulldozer operator clearing the land for a housing development led to the purchase of the property and the creation of the private nonprofit organization that owns the site. The excavation, which has so far unearthed more than 50 mammoths, has explored only 30 percent of the sinkhole. Visitors to the

---

OVERLEAF: *In the North Unit of Badlands National Park near Cedar Pass, erosion has created a veritable fantasyland of peaks, flutes, and crevices. Some areas are washing away at an average of six inches a year.*

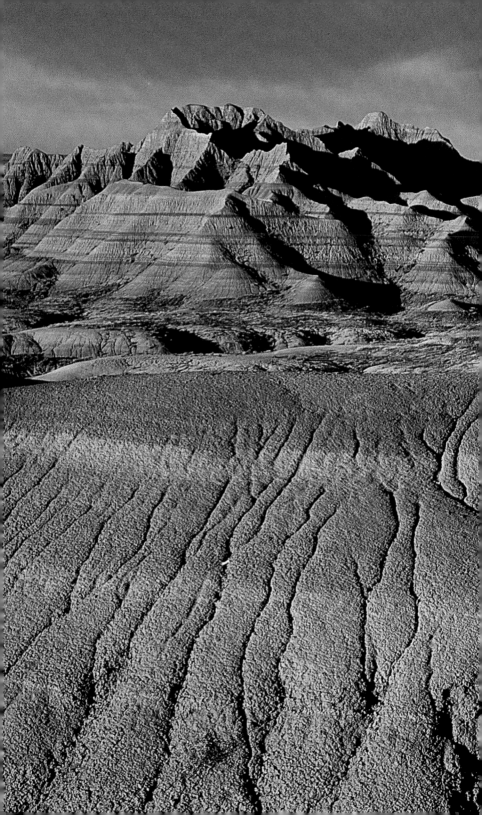

ABOVE: *Black-tailed prairie dogs maintain close family units; here three youngsters emerge from their burrow under an adult's watchful eye.*

site can see a real paleontological dig in progress and tour the small but informative exhibit and visitor center.

Two places chronicle the complex natural and human history of the Hills and surrounding region particularly well. One is the **Museum of Geology❖** on the campus of the South Dakota School of Mines and Technology in Rapid City. The prehistoric remains of marine reptiles, dinosaurs, and other fauna from the fossil-rich Hell Creek Formation are on display here, along with numerous fossilized mammals unearthed in the badlands to the east and outstanding collections of rocks, minerals, and ores. This little museum does a superb job of showcasing South Dakota's wealth as one of the world's fossil hot spots.

The second is the **National Grasslands Visitor Center❖** on Main Street in Wall, about 50 miles east of Rapid City on I-90. Dioramas, artifacts, hands-on objects, videos, and compelling images and graphics teach visitors about the ecology and natural history of the region and the succession of human cultures and societies that have flourished here. Through permanent and temporary exhibits, visitors can explore the various habitats found in the nation's 20 national grasslands, as well as the astonishing biological diversity of the prairies.

BADLANDS NATIONAL PARK: THE NORTH UNIT

East of the Black Hills lie the badlands of the White River, an immense gullied trench that stretches east from the base of the Black Hills. Named

LEFT: *Colors change constantly in the badlands. Here the clear light of sunrise delineates glowing horizontal bands of clay and siltstone.*

for the narrow silt-choked stream that drains these dry reaches, this rumpled, multihued terrain extends some 35 miles north and south and more than 90 miles east, beyond Belvidire. A natural fantasyland of intricately fluted pinnacles, striated scarps, miniature mountain ranges, sculpted knobs, deep arroyos, sharp peaks, and chalk-faced table-flat terraces, this landscape is a graphic illustration of the term *badlands*.

The badlands were formed over a period of 14 million years, as layers of soil accumulated from the mudstones, claystones, and siltstones that washed off the eastern flanks of the Black Hills. Among these softer sediments are harder, erosion-resistant slabs, thin lenses of channel sandstone, and nodules—eroded agglomerations of chemically hardened material. The area's otherworldly topography is a consequence of the softer sediments eroding around and beneath these harder rocks.

Geologists estimate that deposition of these beds began about 37 million years ago, when this region was a broad marshy plain laced with wide, slow-moving streams flowing from the highlands to the west. As

ABOVE: *Because cattlemen exterminated native elk from the Black Hills, herds now in Custer and Wind Cave parks had to be reintroduced.*
LEFT: *Migrating pronghorn, once nearly 40 million strong, were devastated by settlement; today the fleet-footed animals live on protected grasslands, grazing even through the snow.*

the highlands rose, sheets of sediments coursed east, burying everything in their path. Following each uplift was a long period of inactivity, which enabled plant and animal life to return, only to be buried millennia later. Today the striking brightly colored bands—yellows, reds, browns, lavenders, silver grays—that stripe the landscape reflect not only the type of sedimentary material that washed in on each pulse but also the nature of the soils that accumulated before the next inundation. In all, 87 different fossil soils lie exposed in the badlands, each of distinctive hue and content, each an indication of a deposition event.

The most impressive badlands lie within 244,000-acre **Badlands National Park❖,** which is south of I-90 near Wall. The north unit of the park abuts the **Buffalo Gap National Grassland❖,** and the recently acquired south unit lies on the **Pine Ridge Reservation** and is jointly managed by the park service and the Oglala Sioux. Running along the northern edge of the badlands is an extravagantly eroded escarpment known simply as the Wall, which extends eastward from the base of the Black Hills for some 60 miles. Attaining its greatest height at Cedar Pass, where the park maintains a visitor center, the ridge rises some 150 feet above the rolling grasslands to the north and 450 feet above the flat plain to the south. Along the base of the Wall, the land is still changing as huge segments of the scarp continue to break off. Piling atop one another, their formerly horizontal layers tipped, broken, split, and crushed, these soft clay slumps begin eroding almost from the time they hit the ground. Pounded by rain and sliced by runoff and snowmelt, the newest additions to the badlands quickly assume the fantastic and intricately fluted shapes typical of the region.

Among this broken rubble native flora and fauna thrive. The pits and gouges soon become seasonal pools supporting tiny communities of plants and animals. Dotting the bare rocks are a plenitude of colorful wildflowers: purple violets, yellow evening primroses, scarlet globemallow, skunkbush, golden currant, rabbitbrush, sagebrush, and even juniper. On the steeper scarp faces, cliff swallows fashion clusters of their tubular nests, and among small cavities chipmunks, frogs, toads, and salamanders scurry about. The thirteen-lined ground squirrel appears here, as well as prairie rattlers and several other snake species. In the park's grasslands and basins live such animals of the open range as pronghorn, coyotes, bobcat, prairie dogs in their vast underground "towns," mule deer, a few white-tailed deer, and about 500 bison, which were reintroduced in 1963. Also thriving is a small herd of Rocky Mountain bighorn sheep. The species native to these badlands—Audubon's bighorn—was hunted to extinction earlier in this century (the last one was killed in 1926). This reintroduced strain, although not native, seems to be flourishing in the park. The herd, now numbering about 150, is often spotted in the Sage Creek Basin and Stronghold areas.

The most dramatically eroded landscapes are found in the park's northern unit. A good first stop is the **Ben Reifel Visitor Center,** the park's main headquarters at the bottom of Cedar Pass, where visitors can gather information and see an 18-minute video about the area and its intriguing natural history. Near the visitor center, short self-guided hiking trails head into the broken and eroded slumps along the base of the Wall. Along the boardwalk of the informative self-guided **Fossil Exhibit Trail,** a few miles west of the visitor center, replicas of the fossils dug from these clays are interpreted and displayed *in situ.*

These fossils tell a fascinating story of changing climates and ecosystems, of the rise and disappearance of plant and animal life over time. Hugely incomplete, the formations are but a snippet of the story of life on earth, and the cross section in the badlands deals primarily with the rise of mammals. At the bottom, 65-million-year-old Pierre shale—sometimes black, sometimes yellow, sometimes bright red—contains the inhabitants of ancient seas: alligators, sea turtles, and ammonites. Above it, the fluted gray "haystacks" of Chadron claystone have yielded prodigious numbers of fossils of huge rhinolike titanotheres.

The mother lode of fossils, however, is found in the thick strata of the Brule Formation. Ranging in color from yellow-beige to pinkish red, these banded layers represent the entire Oligocene era, from 36 to 23 million years ago. Preserved in the bizarrely eroded rock lie prehistoric oreodonts (sheep-sized ruminants), hippolike Metamynodons, saber-toothed cats, and giant pigs, as well as the ancestors of more familiar creatures: rhinoceroses, camels, and horses.

An excellent way to see the park's striking landscape is to drive the **Badlands Loop Road** (Route 240), which follows the northern rim of the Wall. Alternately skirting the edge or plunging in and out of the trench, the road features a number of scenic overlooks where posted text explains the vista and the significance of certain landmarks.

In the southern portion of the north unit, **Sage Creek Wilderness Area❖** is a 64,250-acre expanse of steeply rolling grasslands and badlands. Scattered juniper and silver sage climb the hillsides, and ash, elm, and cottonwood shade the draws. In summer a large percentage of the more than 200 species of wildflowers in the park bloom in this basin, carpeting the slopes with lavender penstemons and milk vetch, yellow prairie coneflowers, scarlet globemallow, evening primroses, western salsify, and many others. Sage Creek is also one the best birding spots in the badlands, drawing golden eagles and more than eight species of hawks, including northern harriers, Swainson's, and ferruginous hawks. Rock and canyon wrens can be found here, while the woody draws attract many species of sparrows, warblers, and waxwings.

Abutting the wilderness area is another shallow drainage, the **Conata Basin,** where in 1994 the federally endangered black-footed ferret was reintroduced after an absence of more than a decade. A plains weasel once endemic to 12 western states, this little black-masked predator is

ABOVE: *The park's remote south unit, owned jointly with the Oglala, includes Stronghold Table, where Ghost Dance ceremonies of a Native American revival preceded the 1890 massacre at Wounded Knee.*

evolutionarily linked to the prairie dog, its primary prey. As ranchers endeavored to eliminate the prairie dog, long considered an agricultural pest, the ferret was also hunted and poisoned nearly to extinction. Prairie dogs, social creatures that live in extensive underground burrows, or towns, are protected within the park. Whether a complementary ferret population, once native to the Sage Creek and Conata basins, can be increased beyond the threat of extinction remains to be seen.

BADLANDS NATIONAL PARK: THE SOUTH UNIT AND BEYOND

To the south, the landscape flattens out. Groups of sporadic badlands rise up among chalk-sided, flat-topped sod tables. These level grassy terraces, ranging from 12 inches to more than 1,000 feet high, are remnants of an older, higher plain. Today only their sod cover keeps these

RIGHT: *Edible plants in Badlands National Park include soapweed (top), whose fruits can be cooked and eaten once the seeds have been removed, and salsify (bottom), with roots that taste like oysters.*

terraces from eroding away as well. Among the large tablelands that support genuine prairies is **Sheep Mountain Table,** four miles south of the town of Scenic off Route 589 in the northeast corner of the park's southern **Stronghold Unit.** (From the north unit, take Sage Creek Rim Road/Route 590, which runs east under the Wall from the park's Pinnacle entrance to Scenic.) Rising more than 3,000 feet above the grassy plain below, this four-mile-long plateau features a fine mid-grass prairie and a wide variety of prairie flowers. Small stands of juniper grow in the short shallow draws along the escarpment, and from the top, the view of the surrounding badlands is spectacular. Four-wheel-drive vehicles are best for negotiating the jeep track up Sheep Mountain Table, and the road is impassable when wet.

South of Sheep Mountain on BIA Route 27, the park's **White River Visitor Center** presents an informative exhibit and videos on the cul-

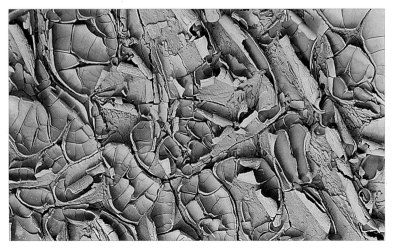

Natural patterns abound in the Stronghold Table area of Badlands National Park: A mosaic of dried mud decorates a creek bottom (above); an encrusted teardrop is actually a fossilized turtleshell (right).

ture of the Oglala and Lakota. The center (open only in summer) is also the jumping-off point for the park's two southern parcels: the 133,000-acre **Stronghold Unit** to the west and the remote **Palmer Creek Unit** to the east. These lands on the Pine Ridge Reservation, added to the park in 1976, are administered jointly by the National Park Service and the Oglala Tribe.

Because the breathtakingly beautiful badlands within these southern units are extremely rugged, four-wheel-drive is a necessity. Topographic maps, available at both visitor centers, are also essential. Vehicles must stay on the few unmarked gravel or primitive backcountry jeep trails, and tribal permission is sometimes required to visit certain areas. In fact, the best way to explore this challenging country is on foot or horseback. The views from Cuny and Stronghold tables—which overlook a panorama of sheer-faced sod tables, fluted hills, and deep canyons—are especially impressive. Stronghold Table was a principal site of the Ghost Dance ceremony, central to a religious cult that attracted Native Americans during the late 1800s. Prophesying an end to white repression, believers proclaimed that specially prepared shirts decorated with sacred symbols could make them impervious to enemy bullets. Their leaders chose this remote tableland because it could be

easily defended should federal troops try to storm it. On a cold December day in 1890, the cult died about 25 miles south of here when troops of the 7th Cavalry caught the Oglala chief Big Foot and his unarmed band at Wounded Knee and massacred some 300 of them.

One way to get an overview of this wild and rugged country is to follow the well-maintained gravel Cuny Table Road (BIA Route 2) along the southern rim of the Stronghold Unit and then turn north on blacktopped 41 to Red Shirt. This route ascends Cuny Table and provides spectacular views of the southern badlands.

ABOVE: *The adaptable coyote thrives throughout the West, its howls punctuating the night.*

RIGHT: *A grove of cottonwoods lightly dusted with snow borders the White River on the Pine Ridge Indian Reservation.*

LACREEK, SANDHILLS, AND THE MISSOURI'S WESTERN BANK

East of the badlands, the buttes, sod tables, and broken land give way to rolling mixed-grass rangeland. About 13 miles southeast of the town of Martin east of Route 73 lies 16,410-acre **Lacreek National Wildlife Refuge❖.** A major nesting area for cormorants and white pelicans, the refuge is also a nesting ground for as many as 3,000 ducks in a good year. Blue-winged teal appear in substantial numbers, as do mallard, shovelers, and gadwalls. Long-billed curlews, American avocets, willets, and upland sandpipers can be spotted along the refuge's shallow, marshy shorelines. Prairie dogs, often on guard atop the mounds that flank the entrances to their dens, display their antics here, and mink, muskrat, beavers, weasels, and even bobcat range throughout the property. A wintering flock of some 200 white trumpeter swans, including 3 to 5 nesting pairs, has become established on the refuge, and during the winter, large numbers of sharp-tailed grouse arrive as well.

Sandwiched between the Pine Ridge and Rosebud reservations, Lacreek occupies a narrow basin on the northern edge of the **Nebraska**

Sandhills. In this vast grass-covered dune field blanketing much of northwestern Nebraska, treeless, hummocky hills cloaked with sparse grasses and yucca roll into the distance. During an extended Pleistocene dry period, sand blew into dunes that were later stabilized by grasses, creating this beautiful, desolate landscape. Although mainly private land, this distinctive country can be experienced in a looping auto tour by heading south on Route 73/61 to Merriman, Nebraska, east on Route 20 for ten miles, and then north on Eli Via County Road into South Dakota and the eastern entrance to the Lacreek refuge at Tuthill.

East of Lacreek and the Rosebud Reservation lie the southern reaches of the Missouri River in South Dakota. Although most of the original Missouri's bottomland lies under a chain of lakes created by giant dams, two remnants of the river as it existed prior to European settlement extend along the South Dakota–Nebraska border. Today they look much as they did when Lewis and Clark first laid eyes on them nearly two centuries ago. Excellent for canoeists, these stretches provide river run-

OVERLEAF:*John Grabill's evocative 1891 photograph is one of the few documents that recorded daily life in a long-gone Brule Sioux village.*

253

ners with an exhilarating experience rich in natural and human history.

The first span of remnant river stretches south from below the Fort Randall Dam about 35 miles to the town of Running Water. Indeed the view from the point below the dam is thought to be precisely what members of the Lewis and Clark expedition saw in the early nineteenth century on their way upstream.

About three-quarters of a mile downstream from the dam is **Eagle Roost** in the **Karl E. Mundt National Wildlife Refuge**❖ (named for the late South Dakota senator and ardent conservationist), which is a staging and nesting area for migrating eagles closed to the public. During the coldest days of winter, the river below the dam is the only open water for many miles, and large numbers of bald eagles gather here to feed on river fish and migrating waterfowl. The huge raptors start appearing in October, and by the end of December—the peak time for viewing—as many as 150 eagles may be stationed on the ice and in trees along the shore. Most will move on by March, following migrating waterfowl to pick off the weak and wounded on the journey north. Visitors in canoes or boats can see eagles up close (the boat ramp is at the end of the point below Fort Randall Dam); the birds can be viewed with binoculars or a spotting scope from the bluff on the Missouri's eastern bank across the river from the refuge.

Downstream the river forms a swift, narrow channel that rolls south through riverbottom cottonwood forests and under high Niobrara chalk bluffs. The Lewis and Clark group traveled this stretch in the waning days of August 1804. In his journal William Clark noted the remarkable abundance of game here: "Vast herds of Baffaloe Deer Elk and Antilopes were seen feeding in every direction as far as the eye of the observer could reach . . . 8 fallow Deer 5 Common & 3 Buffalow killed today." He added with some annoyance: "Muskeetors verry troublesom."

The other reach of remnant Missouri extends 58 miles from below **Gavins Point Dam,** just north of Yankton, to **Ponca State Park**❖ in Nebraska, 23 miles northwest of Sioux City. Although human presence is more apparent here (motorboats, riprap around farm irrigation projects, occasional junked cars along the shore, agricultural fields), the river is a splendid throwback to another time. Surrounded by broad bottomland, cottonwood and willow forests tracing its distant shorelines, the Missouri is laced with sandbars and myriad braided chan-

Above: *Lewis and Clark may well have stood on this bluff near Spring-field, admiring the view and the then free-flowing Missouri River below.*

nels. River maps and other information are available at the **Lewis and Clark Lake Visitor Center❖,** which houses a fine display detailing the river's natural history and the human story of the area. The dam is just south of the junction of Routes 35 and 52, and the visitor center is across the dam on the Nebraska shore.

Here, on the north side of the Missouri, Lewis and Clark climbed to a high prominence shunned by Native Americans, who believed the place to be inhabited by evil spirits. After reaching the top, Clark reported in his journal that he "beheld a most butifull landscape; Numerous herds of buffalow were Seen feeding in various directions; the Plain to North N.W. & N.E. extends without interuption as far as Can be seen." Much has changed across the Northern Plains in the nearly 200 years since those words were written. Although the world they describe is gone, however, it is still as much a part of us as the flesh on our bones—a good thing to keep in mind as we journey into the future.

Overleaf: *Under an evening sky streaked pink and lavender, the broad grasslands of the Great Plains stretch west toward a distant horizon.*

Further Reading About the Northern Plains

Bray, Martha C. *Joseph Nicollet and His Map.* Philadelphia: American Philosophical Society, 1980. An excellent description of the French cartographer's 1838–39 journeys through the uncharted region between the Mississippi and Missouri rivers. Nicollet's lyrical descriptions, in modern translation, form much of the book.

Demaille, Raymond J., Ed. *The Sixth Grandfather. Black Elk's Teachings Given to John G. Neilhardt.* Lincoln: University of Nebraska, 1984. A rereading of the complete set of shorthand notes taken by Neilhardt in his famous interviews with the Oglala Sioux holy man. The book goes well beyond the transcribed notes that formed the basis of Neilhardt's *Black Elk Speaks.* This insightful description illuminates the twilight of the Plains Indian era from the perspective of a Native American who was there.

Devoto, Bernard. *The Journals of Lewis and Clark.* Boston: Houghton Mifflin, 1953. One of the classic edited treatments of the copious notes produced by the two leaders of the 1804–6 Corps of Discovery expedition up the Missouri River and west to the Pacific Ocean. Selected entries are accompanied by helpful footnotes that put recorded events in context.

Froiland, Sven G., and Ronald R. Weedon. *Natural History of the Black Hills and Badlands.* Sioux Falls: The Center for Western Studies, Augustana College, 1990. A solid, compact explanation of the geological origin of the Black Hills and badlands, their human and natural history, and the major environmental challenges that now face the region.

Garland, Hamlin. *A Son of the Middle Border.* 1917. Reprint. New York: Viking Penguin, 1995. One book in a series of personal reminiscences written by a celebrated pioneer-writer about the settling of eastern South Dakota—the Middle Border—during the early 1800s. Garland's prose paintings of the prairie landscape are richly textured in this absorbing personal account by an accomplished storyteller of the closing of the American frontier.

Gruchow, Paul. *Journal of a Prairie Year.* Minneapolis: University of Minnesota Press, 1985. The travels of a first-rate essayist among the scattered remnants of what was once Minnesota's vast tallgrass prairie. Spanning the course of a year in all its seasons, Gruchow's prose is both inspiring and melancholy as it searches out a greater meaning in these shards of a lost landscape.

Manfred, Frederick. *Lord Grizzly.* New York: McGraw Hill, 1954. This classic tale recounts how mountain man Hugh Glass managed to crawl 200 miles to safety after being left for dead by his companions following his mauling by a grizzly bear along the Grand River in northwestern South Dakota. A true story of unbelievable courage and a tenacious will to live, Manfred's treatment—while leavened with a certain measure of bombast—captures a feel for the wildness that was South Dakota in the 1820s.

Further Reading

NORRIS, KATHLEEN. *Dakota, A Spiritual Geography.* New York: Ticknor & Fields, 1993. Essays on the physical and metaphysical landscapes of northwestern South Dakota and the people who have chosen to live there.

NUTE, GRACE LEE. *The Voyageur.* New York: D. Appleton, 1931. An authoritive account of the life and times of the colorful French-Canadian and Native American cargo haulers who plied the rivers, lakes, and trails of northern Minnesota and Canada for the fur industry during the last half of the eighteenth and early years of the nineteenth centuries.

OLSON, SIGURD F. *The Singing Wilderness.* New York: Knopf, 1956. Essays on the wild border-lakes country of northern Minnesota. Olson's prose slips across the page like quick water over smooth stone. A respected biologist and dedicated conservationist, Olson explores both the emotional and natural dimensions of this incomparably beautiful place.

ROLVAAG, OLE E. *Giants in the Earth.* New York: Harper, 1927. The classic saga of the trials and tribulations of a community of Norwegian immigrant settlers in the late 1800s trying to scratch a living out of the prairie wilderness of southeast South Dakota. A novel that convincingly captures both the physical and emotional hardships that the untamed prairie exacted on pioneering Europeans.

ROOSEVELT, THEODORE, *Ranch Life and the Hunting Trail.* New York: Winchester, 1969. Reprint. An account by the twentieth-sixth president of the United States of his experiences in running a ranch in the badlands of North Dakota in the late 1800s. Told in the rambunctious style of an inveterate adventurer, Roosevelt's prose captures the full flavor of western North Dakota at the close of the nineteenth century.

SANSOME, CONSTANCE J. *Minnesota Underfoot.* Stillwater, MN: Voyageur, 1983. The best popular touring guide to the geology of Minnesota is also an excellent resource for anyone wanting to know how Minnesota's landscapes came to be.

TESTER, JOHN R. *Minnesota's Natural Heritage: An Ecological Perspective.* Minneapolis: University of Minnesota Press, 1995. A beautifully illustrated popular guide to the rich natural history of the state from the point of view of a seasoned ecologist who knows his subject well.

WILDER, LAURA INGALLS. *Little House on the Prairie.* 1935. Reprint. New York: HarperCollins, 1990. Perhaps the most famous of Wilder's novels about homesteading on the South Dakota prairie during the late 1800s, based on her childhood and adolescence. Wilder's cheerful take on pioneer life on the prairie provides an interesting contrast to that brooding, painful existence portrayed in Ole Rolvaag's *Giants in the Earth.* The place may be the same, but the view might as well be of two different worlds.

GLOSSARY

arroyo deep channel carved through desert lands by water, especially during sudden storms as floods scour the land

badlands barren, arid area in which soft rock strata are eroded into varied, fantastic forms

biome term used to classify an ecological community according to the specific plant and animal life within

bog wetland formed in glacial kettle holes; acidic nature produces large quantities of peat moss

butte tall, steep-sided tower of rock formed from an eroded plateau; buttes delay inevitable erosional changes because of their hard uppermost layer of rock

coniferous describing the cone-bearing trees of the pine family; usually evergreen

coulee deep ravine, usually dry, worn away by running water

deciduous referring to plants that shed their leaves seasonally and are leafless for part of the year

delta flat, low-lying plain that forms at the mouth of a river as the river slows and deposits sediment gathered farther upstream

dike vertical sheet of rock formed when molten rock cools on its way to the earth's surface and is exposed when surrounding rock erodes

draw shallow gully

endemic having originated in and being restricted to one particular environment

escarpment cliff or steep rock face, formed by faulting or fracturing of the earth's crust, that separates two comparatively level land surfaces

esker long, winding rise of gravel and sand that marks the trail where a river once flowed beneath a glacier

fen any lowland covered wholly or partly with water

floodplain flat area along the course of a stream that is subject to periodic flooding and deposition of the sediment the stream has been carrying

glacial till unsorted rock debris, usually of a wide range of sizes, deposited directly from the ice sheet without reworking by streams

hogback sharply defined ridge produced by the erosion of highly angled rock layers, one of which is more resistant than the others

hoodoo natural column of rock often formed into fantastic shapes; found in western North America

igneous referring to rock formed by cooled or hardened lava or magma

kame cone-shaped hill of rock debris deposited by glacial meltwater

karst area of land lying over limestone that is dotted with sinkholes, underground streams, and caves formed by the erosion of limestone by rainwater

kettle hole glacial depression that, when fed by groundwater and precipitation, often evolves into a bog

laccolith underground body of lens-shaped igneous rock that has squeezed between rock layers forcing the strata above into a dome shape

lateral moraine hill or ridge of debris (rock, sand, gravel, silt, and clay) deposited along a retreating or advancing glacier's side

massif zone of the earth's crust raised or depressed by plate movement and bounded by faults

mesa isolated, relatively flat-topped natural elevation more extensive than a butte and less extensive than a plateau

metamorphic referring to a rock that has been changed into its present state after being subjected to heat, pressure, or chemical change

oxbow lake lake created where a meandering river overflows, forming a crescent-shaped body of water; called an oxbow because its curved shape looks like the U-shaped harness frame that fits around an ox's neck

pothole bowl-shaped depression left by a chunk of glacial ice buried in soil; when ice melts, water fills the pothole creating either a lake or a marsh

prairie temperate grassland supporting an extensive variety of grasses; occurs in areas where there are distinct seasonal variations in climate

riparian relating to the bank of a natural watercourse, lake, or tidewater

savanna tropical grassland marked by clumps of grasses and widely scattered tree growth; occurs in areas where a prolonged dry season alternates with a rainy season

scarp line of steep cliffs formed by erosion

sedge family of grasslike plants found in brackish swamps and marshes

sedimentary referring to rocks formed from deposits of eroded debris such as gravel, sand, mud, silt, or peat

seep small spring or pool fed by groundwater

sinkhole funnel-shaped hole formed where water has collected in the cracks of limestone, dissolved the rock, and carried it away; also formed when roofs of caves collapse

slough swampy, backwater area, river inlet, or creek in a marsh or tidal flat

stalactite icicle-shaped piece of dripstone formed when water containing dissolved limestone drips from the roof of a cave and evaporates, leaving the mineral formation

stalagmite spire formed when water drips onto a cave floor and deposits minerals dissolved in the water

swale moist, low area in a tract of land; usually more dense in vegetation than the surrounding areas

tableland large area of elevated, level land

talus rock debris that accumulates at the base of a cliff

terminal moraine final deposit of rock and debris that forms at a glacier's farthest leading edge and is left behind as the glacier retreats

timberline boundary that marks the upper limit of forest growth on a mountain or in high latitudes; beyond the boundary, temperatures are too cold to support tree growth

vulcanism processes associated with the creation of volcanoes and their subsequent geologic activities

wetland area of land covered or saturated with groundwater; includes swamps, marshes, and bogs

LAND MANAGEMENT RESOURCES

The following public and private organizations are among the important administrators of the preserved and protected areas described in this volume. Brief explanations of the various legal and legislative designations of these areas follow.

MANAGING AGENCIES

Minnesota Division of Fish and Wildlife
Administers wildlife management areas and scientific and natural areas. Issues hunting and fishing licenses. Part of the Department of Natural Resources.

Minnesota Division of Forestry
Manages 4.4 million acres within 55 state forests. Land is managed for recreation, timber, and hunting. Part of the Department of Natural Resources.

Minnesota Division of Parks and Recreation
Manages 200,000 acres of state recreational land within 78 state parks, recreation areas, and waysides. Part of the Department of Natural Resources.

National Audubon Society (NAS) Private organization
International nonprofit conservation, lobbying, and educational organization that owns a private network of wildlife sanctuaries. Strives to protect natural ecosystems through grassroots organization and education.

National Park Service (NPS) Department of the Interior
Manages national parks, monuments, and preserves to protect landscape, natural and historic artifacts, and wildlife. Administers historic and national landmarks, national seashores, wild and scenic rivers, and national trails.

The Nature Conservancy (TNC) Private organization
International nonprofit organization that owns some 1,300 sanctuaries worldwide. Aims to preserve significant plants, animals, and natural communities. Some areas managed by other groups, some by the Conservancy.

North Dakota Forest Service
Manages 12,000 acres in one state forest and numerous forestlands. Forest is managed for recreation, timber production, and hunting.

North Dakota Game and Fish Department
Manages some 177,000 acres of wildlife management areas for conservation of wildlife, hunting, and fishing. Issues state hunting and fishing licenses.

North Dakota Parks and Recreation Department
Manages 19,271 acres of land within 11 state parks, 5 recreation areas, 9 nature preserves, and 3 state historic sites.

South Dakota Division of Parks and Recreation
Maintains 92,710 acres of land within 12 state parks, 25 recreation areas, and 36 lakeside use areas. Part of the Game, Fish and Parks Department.

South Dakota Division of Wildlife
Manages 147,151 acres of wildlife land for conservation of wildlife, and hunting. Part of Game, Fish and Parks Department.

U.S. Fish and Wildlife Service (USFWS) Department of the Interior
Principal federal agency responsible for national wildlife refuges and fish

hatcheries and programs for migratory birds and endangered species.

U.S. Forest Service (USFS) Department of Agriculture
Administers 190 million acres of national forests and grasslands. Balances commercial uses (grazing, mining, and logging) with conservation needs.

DESIGNATIONS

National Forest
Large acreage managed for the use of forests, watersheds, wildlife, and recreation by the public and private sectors. Managed by the USFS.

National Game Preserve
Federal land managed as part of the National Wildlife Refuge System with designated areas for big game. No hunting. Managed by the USFWS.

National Grassland
Federal land where more than 80 percent of the canopy cover is dominated by grasses. May encompass private holdings. Managed by the USFS.

National Monument
Nationally significant landmark, structure, object, or area of scientific or historic significance. Managed by the NPS.

National Park
Primitive or wilderness area with scenery and natural wonders so outstanding it has been preserved by the federal government. Managed by the NPS.

National Wildlife Refuge
Public land set aside for wild animals; protects migratory waterfowl, endangered and threatened species, and native plants. Managed by the USFWS.

Natural Area
Area designated and preserved in its natural state as an example of the natural history of the United States. Managed by individual states.

Nature Preserve
Area that protects specific natural resources. Hunting, fishing, and mining may be permitted. Managed by the NPS and local or state authorities.

Scientific and Natural Area
Reserve that protects rare and endangered species, geological forms, and native plant and animal communities. Managed by individual states.

Recreation Area
Site established to conserve for recreational purposes an area of scenic, national, or historic interest. Powerboats, dirt and mountain bikes, and ORVs allowed with restrictions. Managed by the NPS or individual states.

Wilderness Area
Area with particular ecological, geological, scientific, scenic, or historic value that has been set aside in its natural condition to be preserved as wild land; limited recreational use is permitted. Managed by BLM and NPS.

Wildlife Management Area
Land managed to protect wildlife. Aside from seasonal restrictions, hunting, fishing, and public access are allowed. Managed by individual states.

NATURE TRAVEL

The following is a selection of national and local organizations that sponsor nature-related travel activities or can provide specialized regional travel information.

NATIONAL

National Audubon Society
700 Broadway
New York, NY 10003
(212) 979-3000
Offers a wide range of ecological field studies, tours, and cruises throughout the United States

National Wildlife Federation
1400 16th Street NW
Washington, D.C. 20036
(703) 790-4363
Offers training in environmental education, wildlife camp and teen adventures, conservation summits with nature walks, field trips, and classes

The Nature Conservancy
1815 North Lynn St.
Arlington, VA 22209
(703) 841-5300
Offers a variety of excursions from regional and state offices. May include hiking, backpacking, canoeing, horseback riding. Call to locate state offices

Sierra Club Outings
85 2nd St. 2nd fl.
San Francisco, CA 94105
(415) 977-5630
Offers tours of different lengths for all ages throughout the United States. Outings may include backpacking, hiking, biking, skiing, and water excursions

Smithsonian Study Tours and Seminars
1100 Jefferson Dr. SW, MRC 702
Washington, D.C. 20560
(202) 357-4700
Offers extended tours, cruises, research expeditions, and seminars throughout the United States

REGIONAL

Minnesota Office of Tourism
100 Metro Sq.
121 E. 7th Pl.
St. Paul, MN 55101
(612) 296-5029
Provides specific information for travelers as well as general tourism brochures for out-of-state visitors

North Dakota Tourism Department
604 E. Boulevard
Bismarck, ND 58505
(701) 328-2525
(800) 435-5663
Offers vacation planning guides and state highway maps and can answer specific questions regarding travel and recreation

South Dakota Department of Tourism
711 E. Wells Ave.
Pierre, SD 57501
(800) 732-5682 (for brochures)
(800) 952-3625 (for specific questions)
Travelers can call or write for specific information or to order state maps and vacation guides

Institute of Range and the American Mustang
Box 432
Hot Springs, SD 57747
(605) 745-5955
(800) 252-6652
Offers summer tours for wildlife and wildflower viewing and photography and tepee rentals for camping; Black Hills Wild Horse Sanctuary on site

HOW TO USE THIS SITE GUIDE

The following site information guide will assist you in planning your tour of the natural areas of Minnesota, North Dakota, and South Dakota. Sites set in boldface and followed by the symbol ❖ in the text are here organized alphabetically by state. Each entry is followed by the mailing address (sometimes different from the street address) and phone number of the immediate managing office, plus brief notes and a list of facilities and activities available. (A key appears on each page.)

Information on hours of operation, seasonal closings, and fees is often not listed, as these vary from season to season and year to year. Please bear in mind that responsibility for the management of some sites may change. Call well in advance to obtain maps, brochures, and pertinent, up-to-date information that will help you plan your adventures in the Northern Plains.

Each site entry in the guide includes the address and phone number of its immediate managing agency. Many of these sites are under the stewardship of a forest or park ranger or supervised from a small nearby office. Hence, in many cases, those sites will be difficult to contact directly, and it is preferable to call the managing agency.

The following umbrella organizations can provide general information for individual natural sites, as well as the area as a whole:

MINNESOTA

Minnesota Division of Fish and Wildlife
500 Lafayette Rd.
St. Paul, MN 55155
(612) 297-1308

Minnesota Division of Forestry
500 Lafayette Rd.
St. Paul, MN 55155
(612) 296-4491

Minnesota Division of Parks and Recreation
500 Lafayette Rd.
St. Paul, MN 55155
(612) 296-9223

NORTH DAKOTA

North Dakota Parks and Recreation Department
1835 Bismarck Expwy.
Bismarck, ND 58504
(701) 328-5370

North Dakota State Forest Service
1st and Brander
Bottineau, ND 58318
(701) 228-5422

North Dakota State Game and Fish Department
100 N. Bismarck Expy.
Bismarck, ND 58501
(701) 328-6300

SOUTH DAKOTA

South Dakota Division of Parks and Recreation
523 East Capitol
Pierre, SD 57501
(605) 773-3391

South Dakota Game, Fish, and Parks Department
523 East Capitol
Pierre, SD 57501
(605) 773-3387

REGIONAL

National Park Service
1709 Jackson St.
Omaha, NE 68102
(402) 221-3431

U.S. Fish and Wildlife Service—Region 6
134 Union Blvd.
PO Box 25486
Denver, CO 80225
(303) 236-7905

U.S. Forest Service—Region 1
Federal Bldg.
200 E. Broadway
PO Box 7669
Missoula, MT 59807
(402) 329-3316

U.S. Forest Service—Region 9
310 W. Wisconsin
Ste. 500
Milwaukee, WI 53202
(414) 297-3600

MINNESOTA

AGASSIZ DUNES SCIENTIFIC AND NATURAL AREA
Minnesota Div. of Fish and Wildlife
Scientific and Natural Areas Program
Box 7, DNR Bldg., 500 Lafayette Rd.
St. Paul, MN 55155-4007
(612) 296-3344;
(612) 331-0750 (TNC)   **BW, H**

ALEXANDER RAMSEY CITY PARK
City of Redwood Falls, Parks Dept.
PO Box 10
Redwood Falls, MN 56283
(507) 637-5755   **BW, C, CK, F, H,
                              MT, PA, T, XC**

BANNING STATE PARK
Minnesota Div. of Parks and Recreation
PO Box 643,
Sandstone, MN 55072
(612) 245-2668
    Intermittent seasonal ranger-led activities
                    **BW, C, CK, F, H, I,
                      MT, PA, RA, T, XC**

BEAVER CREEK VALLEY STATE PARK
Minnesota Div. of Parks and Recreation
Rte. 2, Box 57
Caledonia, MN 55921
(507) 724-2107
    Includes a nature center and children's
    wading pool   **BW, C, F, H,
                            I, MT, PA, T, XC**

BIG STONE LAKE STATE PARK
Minnesota Div. of Parks and Recreation
RR 1, Box 153
Ortonville, MN 56278
(612) 839-3663 (April–December)
    Park closed January–March
                BW, C, F, H, MT, PA, S, T

BIG STONE NATIONAL WILDLIFE REFUGE
U.S. Fish and Wildlife Service
25 NW 2nd St.
Ortonville, MN 56278
(612) 839-3700   **BT, BW, CK, F,
                            H, MT, T, XC**

BLUE MOUNDS STATE PARK
Minnesota Div. of Parks and Recreation
Rte. 1, Box 52
Luverne, MN 56156
(507) 283-4892   **BW, C, CK, F, GS, H,
                            MT, PA, RC, S, T, XC**

BLUESTEM PRAIRIE SCIENTIFIC AND NATURAL AREA
Minnesota Div. of Fish and Wildlife
Scientific and Natural Areas Program
Box 7, DNR Bldg., 500 Lafayette Rd.
St. Paul, MN 55155-4007
(218) 498-2679
(Bluestem Prairie office, TNC)
(218) 498-2124 (Buffalo River State Park)
    Reservations necessary to watch prairie
    chickens at leks in early spring   **BW, H**

BONANZA PRAIRIE SCIENTIFIC AND NATURAL AREA
Minnesota Div. of Fish and Wildlife
Scientific and Natural Areas Program
Box 7, DNR Bldg., 500 Lafayette Rd.
St. Paul, MN 55155-4007
(612) 296-3344; (612) 839-3663
(Big Stone Lake State Park)
                                            H

BOUNDARY WATERS CANOE AREA WILDERNESS
Superior National Forest
PO Box 338
Duluth, MN 55801
(218) 720-5324   **BW, C, CK, F,
                            H, I, TG, XC**

BUFFALO RIVER STATE PARK
Minnesota Div. of Parks and Recreation
Rte. 2, Box 256
Glyndon, MN 56547
(218) 498-2124   **BW, C, F, GS, H,
                            I, MT, PA, RA, S, T, XC**

BUTTERWORT CLIFFS SCIENTIFIC AND NATURAL AREA
Minnesota Div. of Fish and Wildlife
Scientific and Natural Areas Program
Box 7, DNR Bldg., 500 Lafayette Rd.
St. Paul, MN 55155-4007
(612) 296-3344; (218) 387-1543
(Cascade River State Park)
    Closed May 1–August 15; permit required
    from park headquarters to visit   **BW**

CASCADE RIVER STATE PARK
Minnesota Div. of Parks and Recreation
HC 3, Box 450, Lutsen, MN 55612-9705
(218) 387-1543   **BW, C, F, GS,
                            H, I, MT, PA, T, XC**

CHENGWATANA STATE FOREST
Minnesota Div. of Forestry
Rte. 2, Box 386B, Hinckley, MN 55037
(612) 384-6146   **BW, C, CK, F,
                            H, HR, MB, PA, S, T, XC**

BT Bike Trails
BW Bird-watching
C Camping
CK Canoeing, Kayaking
DS Downhill Skiing
F Fishing
GS Gift Shop
H Hiking
HR Horseback Riding
I Information Center

CHIPPEWA NATIONAL FOREST
U.S. Forest Service
Rte. 3, Box 244, Cass Lake, MN 56633
(218) 335-8600, (218) 335-8632 (TTY)
BT, BW, C, CK, F, H, HR, I,
MB, MT, PA, RA, S, T, TG, XC

CHIPPEWA PRAIRIE
The Nature Conservancy
Minnesota Chapter
1313 Fifth St., SE
Minneapolis, MN 55414-1588
(612) 331-0750   BW

**FELTON PRAIRIE SCIENTIFIC
AND NATURAL AREA**
Minnesota Div. of Fish and Wildlife
Scientific and Natural Areas Program
Box 7, DNR Bldg., 500 Lafayette Rd.
St. Paul, MN 55155-4007
(612) 296-3344; (612) 331-0750 (TNC)
Includes Bicentennial Prairie, Blazing
Star Prairie, and Shrike Units   BW

FERTILE SAND HILLS
Agassiz Environmental Learning Center
PO Box 388, Fertile, MN 56540
(218) 945-3129   BW, C, CK, H,
I, MT, PA, T, XC

FLANDRAU STATE PARK
Minnesota Div. of Parks and Recreation
1300 Summit Ave., New Ulm, MN 56073
(507) 354-3519
Group barracks available   BW, C, CK,
F, GS, H, I, L, MT, PA, S, T, XC

FORT SNELLING STATE PARK
Minnesota Div. of Parks and Recreation
Rte. 5 and Post Road
St. Paul, MN 55111
(612) 725-2390   BT, BW, CK, F, H, MT,
PA, RA, S, T, XC

**FRENCHMAN'S BLUFF SCIENTIFIC AND
NATURAL AREA**
Minnesota Div. of Fish and Wildlife
Scientific and Natural Areas Program
Box 7, DNR Bldg., 500 Lafayette Rd.
St. Paul, MN 55155-4007
(612) 296-3344;
(612) 331-0750 (TNC)   BW

FRONTENAC STATE PARK
Minnesota Div. of Parks and Recreation
23223 County 28 Blvd.
Lake City, MN 55041
(612) 345-3401   BW, C, F, GS, H,
MT, PA, RA, T, XC

**GEORGE H. CROSBY–MANITOU
STATE PARK**
Minnesota Div. of Parks and Recreation
474 Rte. 61E, Silver Bay, MN 55614
(218) 226-3539   BW, C, F, H, MT, PA, T

GLACIAL LAKES STATE PARK
Minnesota Div. of Parks and Recreation
Rte. 2, Box 126, Starbuck, MN 56381
(612) 239-2860   BT, BW, C, CK, F, H,
HR, I, MB, MT, PA, S, T, XC

GOOSEBERRY FALLS STATE PARK
Minnesota Div. of Parks and Recreation
1300 Rte. 61E, Two Harbors, MN 55616
(218) 834-3855   BW, C, F, GS, H, I,
MB, MT, PA, RA, T, XC

GOOSE CREEK NATURAL AREA
Wild River State Park
39755 Park Trail, Center City, MN 55012
(612) 583-2125   BW

**GRAND PORTAGE
NATIONAL MONUMENT**
National Park Service, PO Box 668
Grand Marais, MN 55604
(218) 387-2788 (headquarters and TDD)
(218) 475-2202 (monument)
BW, GS, H, I, MT,
PA, RA, T, TG, XC

GRAND PORTAGE STATE PARK
Minnesota Div. of Parks and Recreation
HCR 1, Box 7, Grand Portage, MN 55605
(218) 475-2360
Day use only; tribal license as well as
state license required for fishing
BW, CK, F, GS, H, I, MT, PA, T

GRANITE FALLS MEMORIAL PARK
City of Granite Falls
885 Prentice St., Granite Falls, MN 56241
(612) 564-3011   C, F, H, MT, PA, T

HAWK RIDGE
Duluth Audubon Society
c/o Biology Dept., Univ. of Minnesota
Duluth Branch, Duluth, MN 55812
(218) 525-6930   BW, H

**HELEN ALLISON SAVANNA
SCIENTIFIC AND NATURAL AREA**
Minnesota Div. of Fish and Wildlife
Scientific and Natural Areas Program
Box 7, DNR Bldg., 500 Lafayette Rd.
St. Paul, MN 55155-4007
(612) 296-3344; (612) 331-0750 (TNC) BW

L	Lodging	**PA**	Picnic Areas	**RC**	Rock Climbing	**TG**	Tours, Guides
MB	Mountain Biking	**RA**	Ranger-led Activities	**S**	Swimming	**XC**	Cross-country Skiing
MT	Marked Trails			**T**	Toilets		

269

Hemlock Ravine Scientific and Natural Area
Minnesota Div. of Fish and Wildlife
Scientific and Natural Areas Program
Box 7, DNR Bldg., 500 Lafayette Rd.
St. Paul, MN 55155-4007
(612) 296-3344; (218) 384-4610
(Jay Cooke State Park)   **BW, H**

Hole-in-the-Mountain Prairie
The Nature Conservancy
Minnesota Chapter, 1313 Fifth St., SE
Minneapolis, MN 55414-1588
(612) 331-0750   **BW**

Inspiration Peak
Lake Carlos State Park
2601 County Rd. 38 NE, Carlos, MN 56319
(612) 852-7200   **BW, H, MT, PA, T**

International Wolf Center
1396 Rte. 169, Ely, MN 55731-8129
(218) 365-4695; (800) 359-9653
    Admission fee; additional fee for some
    programs; open Friday, Saturday, and
    Sunday October–April; open daily rest
    of year   **BW, C, CK, GS, H, I, MB, PA,
                      RA, T, TG, XC**

Interstate State Park
Minnesota Div. of Parks and Recreation
PO Box 254, Taylors Falls, MN 55084
(612) 465-5711
    Tours and gift shop summer season
    only   **BW, C, CK, F, GS, H,
                   MT, PA, RC, T, TG**

Ironworld Discovery Center
PO Box 392, Chisholm, MN 55719
(218) 254-3323
(218) 254-3325 (research center)
    Admission fee   **BT, C, GS, H, I, MT,
                           PA, RA, T, TG, XC**

Itasca State Park
Minnesota Div. of Parks and Recreation
HC 05, Box 4, Lake Itasca, MN 56470
(218) 266-3304; (218) 266-2114
    Includes museum; seasonal lodging;
    group camps   **BT, BW, C, CK, F, GS, H,
                          I, L, MT, PA, RA, S, T, TG, XC**

Jay Cooke State Park
Minnesota Div. of Parks and Recreation
500 E. Rte. 210
Carlton, MN 55718
(218) 384-4610   **BT, BW, C, F, H, HR,
                         I, MB, MT, PA, RA, T, XC**

Lac qui Parle State Park
Minnesota Div. of Parks and Recreation
Rte. 5, Box 74A
Montevideo, MN 56265
(612) 752-4736   **BT, BW, C, CK, F, GS,
                         H, HR, I, MB, MT, PA, S, T, XC**

Lac qui Parle Wildlife Management Area
Minnesota Div. of Fish and Wildlife
14040 20th St., NW
Watson, MN 56295
(612) 734-4451
    Group tours by prearrangement
                         BW, F, H, XC

Maplewood State Park
Minnesota Div. of Parks and Recreation
Rte. 3, Box 422
Pelican Rapids, MN 56572
(218) 863-8383   **BW, C, CK, F, H,
                         HR, L, MT, S, T, XC**

Minneopa State Park
Minnesota Div. of Parks and Recreation
RR 9, Box 143
Mankato, MN 56001-8219
(507) 389-5464
    Includes Historic Seppmann Windmill
    and Minneopa Twin Falls
                         **BW, C, CK, F, GS, H,
                          I, MT, PA, S, T, XC**

Minnesota Valley National Wildlife Refuge
U.S. Fish and Wildlife Service
3815 E. 80th St.
Bloomington, MN 55425
(612) 335-2323
(612) 335-2299 (recorded information)
                         **BW, GS, H, HR, I,
                          MB, MT, RA, T, TG, XC**

Mystery Cave
Forestville State Park
Rte. 2, Box 128
Preston, MN 55965
(507) 352-5111   **PA, RA, T, TG**

Nerstrand Big Woods State Park
Minnesota Div. of Parks and Recreation
9700 170th St.
Nerstrand, MN 55053
(507) 334-8848   **BW, C, GS, H,
                         I, MT, PA, T, XC**

BT Bike Trails
BW Bird-watching
C Camping
CK Canoeing, Kayaking
DS Downhill Skiing
F Fishing
GS Gift Shop
H Hiking
HR Horseback Riding
I Information Center

O. L. Kipp State Park
Minnesota Div. of Parks and Recreation
Rte. 4, Winona, MN 55987
(507) 643-6849   **BW, C, H, MT, PA, T, XC**

Ordway Prairie
The Nature Conservancy
Minnesota Chapter
1313 Fifth St. SE
Minneapolis, MN 55414-1588
(612) 331-0750   **BW**

Pembina Trails Preserve Scientific and Natural Area
Minnesota Div. of Fish and Wildlife
Scientific and Natural Areas Program
Box 7, DNR Bldg., 500 Lafayette Rd.
St. Paul MN 55155-4007
(612) 296-3344; (612) 331-0750 (TNC) **BW**

Pipestone National Monument
National Park Service
PO Box 727, Pipestone, MN 56164
(507) 825-546 **BW, GS, H, I, MT, PA, T, TG**

Plover Prairie
The Nature Conservancy
Minnesota Chapter
1313 Fifth St., SE
Minneapolis, MN 55414-1588
(612) 331-0750   **BW**

Prairie Coteau Scientific and Natural Area
Minnesota Div. of Fish and Wildlife
Scientific and Natural Areas Program
Box 7, DNR Bldg., 500 Lafayette Rd.
St. Paul, MN 55155-4007
(612) 296-3344   **BW, H**

Red Lake Peatlands
Minnesota Div. of Fish and Wildlife
Scientific and Natural Areas Program
Box 7, DNR Bldg., 500 Lafayette Rd.
St. Paul, MN 55155-4007
(218) 755-3953; (612) 296-3344
Camping in designated areas only;
snowmobile trails   **BW, C, MT, S, XC**

Rothsay Prairie Wildlife Management Area
Minnesota Div. of Fish and Wildlife
1221 East Fir Ave.
Fergus Falls, MN 56537
(218) 739-7576   **BW, H**

Saint Croix National Scenic Riverway
National Park Service
PO Box 708, St. Croix Falls, WI 54024
(715) 483-3284   **BW, C, CK, F, H, I, MT, PA, RA, T, TG, XC**

Saint Croix State Park
Minnesota Div. of Parks and Recreation
Rte. 3, Box 450
Hinckley, MN 55037
(612) 384-6591; (612) 384-6615
Lodging and camping reservation
recommended; horse camp; snowmobile trails   **BT, BW, C, CK, F, GS, H, HR, I, L, MB, MT, PA, RA, S, T, XC**

Sand Dunes State Forest
Uncas Dunes Scientific and Natural Area
Minnesota Div. of Forestry
12969 Fremont Ave.
Zimmerman, MN 55398
(612) 856-4826; (612) 689-7100
    BW, C, F, H, HR, MB, MT, PA, S, T, XC

Scenic State Park
Minnesota Div. of Parks and Recreation
HCR 2, Box 17
Bigfork, MN 56628
(218) 743-3362
    BT, BW, C, CK, F, GS, H, I, L, MB, MT, PA, RA, S, T, TG, XC

Split Rock Lighthouse
Minnesota Historical Society
2010 Rte. 61E
Two Harbors, MN 55616
(218) 226-4372 (Historical Society at Lighthouse)
(218) 226-3065 (Split Rock Lighthouse
State Park)   **BW, C, CK, F, GS, H, I, MB, MT, PA, T, TG, XC**

Superior Hiking Trail
Superior Hiking Trail Association
PO Box 4, Two Harbors, MN 55616
(218) 834-2700   **BW, C, F, GS, H, I, MT**

Superior National Forest
U.S. Forest Service
PO Box 338
Duluth, MN 55801
(218) 720-5324 **BT, BW, C, CK, F, H, HR, MB, MT, PA, RA, S, T, XC**

L	Lodging	**PA**	Picnic Areas	**RC**	Rock Climbing	**TG**	Tours, Guides
MB	Mountain Biking	**RA**	Ranger-led Activities	**S**	Swimming	**XC**	Cross-country Skiing
MT	Marked Trails			**T**	Toilets		

TEMPERANCE RIVER STATE PARK
Minnesota Div. of Parks and Recreation
PO Box 33
Schroeder, MN 55613
(218) 663-7476   BW, C, CK, F, GS, H, I,
                      MT, PA, RC, T, XC

TETTEGOUCHE STATE PARK
Minnesota Div. of Parks and Recreation
474 Rte 61E
Silver Bay, MN 55614
(218) 226-3539   BW, C, CK, F, GS, H, I, L,
                      MT, PA, RC, S, T, XC

**UPPER MISSISSIPPI RIVER NATIONAL
WILDLIFE AND FISH REFUGE**
U.S. Fish and Wildlife Service
51 East 4th St.
Winona, MN 55987
(507) 454-7351
        BT, BW, C, CK, F, H, I, S, TG, XC
UPPER SIOUX AGENCY STATE PARK
Minnesota Div. of Parks and Recreation
Rte. 2, Box 92
Granite Falls, MN 56241
(612) 564-4777   BW, C, CK, F, GS, H,
                      HR, I, MT, PA, T

VOYAGEURS NATIONAL PARK
National Park Service
3131 Rte. 53,International Falls, MN 56649
(218) 283-9821   BW, C, CK, F, GS, H, I,
                 L, MT, PA, RA, S, T, TG, XC

**WEAVER DUNES PRESERVE SCIENTIFIC
AND NATURAL AREA**
Minnesota Div. of Fish and Wildlife
Scientific and Natural Areas Program
Box 7, DNR Bldg., 500 Lafayette Rd.
St. Paul, MN 55155-4007
(612) 296-3344
(612) 331-0750 (TNC)   BW, H

WHITEWATER STATE PARK
Minnesota Div. of Parks and Recreation
Rte. 1, Box 256
Altura, MN 55910
(507) 932-3007   BW, C, F, GS, H, I, MT,
                      PA, RA, S, T, TG, XC

**WHITEWATER WILDLIFE
MANAGEMENT AREA**
Minnesota Div. of Fish and Wildlife
RR 2, Box 333, Altura, MN 55910
(507) 932-4133   BW, F, H, I

WILD RIVER STATE PARK
Minnesota Div. of Parks and Recreation
39755 Park Trail
Center City, MN 55012
(612) 583-2125; (612) 583-2925
Biking on park roads only
                      BW, C, CK, F, GS, H, HR,
                      I, L, MT, PA, RA, T, TG, XC

NORTH DAKOTA

ALKALI LAKE
U.S. Fish and Wildlife Service
1 First St. SW, PO Box E
Kulm, ND 58456
(701) 647-2866 (USFWS)
(701) 328-6300 (NDGF)   BW, H

ALKALI LAKE SANCTUARY
National Audubon Society
Rte. 1, Box 79A
Spiritwood, ND 58481
(701) 252-3822
Primitive camping
                      BW, C, CK, H, HR, I, PA, TG

BULLION BUTTE
U.S. Forest Service
Medora Ranger District
161 21st St. W
Dickinson, ND 58601-3135
(701) 225-5151   BW, C, H, HR, MB

BURNING COAL VEIN
U.S. Forest Service
Medora Ranger District
161 21st St. W
Dickinson, ND 58601-3135
(701) 25-5151   BT, BW, C, H, HR,
                      MB, PA, T, XC
**CHASE LAKE NATIONAL
WILDLIFE REFUGE**
U.S. Fish and Wildlife Service
Chase Lake Wetland Management District
5924 19th St., SE
Woodworth, ND 58496
(701) 752-4218
Information here for Woodworth Water-
fowl Production Area   BW

CROSS RANCH NATURE PRESERVE
The Nature Conservancy
2000 Schafer St., Ste. B
Bismarck, ND 58501-1204
(701) 222-8464   BW, H, MT

BT	Bike Trails	**CK**	Canoeing, Kayaking	**F**	Fishing	**HR**	Horseback Riding
BW	Bird-watching			**GS**	Gift Shop		
C	Camping	**DS**	Downhill Skiing	**H**	Hiking	**I**	Information Center

CROSS RANCH STATE PARK
North Dakota Parks and Recreation Dept.
1835 E. Bismarck Expwy.
Bismarck, ND 58504
(701) 794-3731
  No electrical hookups in campground
          BW, C, CK, F, H, I, MT, PA, RA, T, XC

DES LACS NATIONAL WILDLIFE REFUGE
U.S. Fish and Wildlife Service
PO Box 578,
Kenmare, ND 58746
(701) 385-4046
  11-mile auto-tour route; best time to visit
  May–October; winter travel difficult;
  most wildlife gone in winter
          BW, CK, H, I, MB, PA, T, XC

DEVILS LAKE
Devils Lake Area
Chamber of Commerce
Rte. 2E, PO Box B 79
Devils Lake, ND 58301
(701) 662-4903   **BT, BW, C, CK, DS, F, GS,**
          H, I, L, MT, PA, RA, S, T, TG, XC

GEORGE LAKE
U.S. Fish and Wildlife Service
Long Lake NWR Complex
12000 353rd St., SE
Moffitt, ND 58560
(701) 387-4397   **BW, PA**

GRAHAMS ISLAND STATE PARK
North Dakota Parks and Recreation Dept.
c/o Devils Lake State Park
Rte. 1, Box 165
Devils Lake, ND 58301
(701) 766-4015
  Tours by prearrangement   **BW, C, F, GS,**
          H, I, MT, PA, RA, T, TG, XC

HOMEN STATE FOREST
North Dakota Forest Service
First and Brander Sts.
Bottineau, ND 58318
(701) 228-3700   **BW, C, F, H, PA, T**

ICELANDIC STATE PARK
North Dakota Parks and
Recreation Dept.
13571 Rte. 5
Cavalier, ND 58220
(701) 265-4561   **BW, C, F, GS, H,**
          I, MT, PA, S, T, XC

INTERNATIONAL PEACE GARDEN
Rte. 1, Box 116
Dunseith, ND 58329
(701) 263-4390   **BT, BW, C, GS,**
          H, I, PA, T, TG

J. CLARK SALYER NATIONAL WILDLIFE REFUGE
U.S. Fish and Wildlife Service
PO Box 66, Upham, ND 58789
(701) 768-2548
  Auto-tour route may be closed in wet or
  snowy weather   **BW, CK, F, H, PA, T**

JAY V. WESSELS WILDLIFE MANAGEMENT AREA
North Dakota Game and Fish Dept.
RR 5, Box 281 B
Devils Lake, ND 58301
(701) 662-3617   **BW, H, HR, MT**

JOHNSON'S GULCH WILDLIFE MANAGEMENT AREA
North Dakota Game and Fish Dept.
Spiritwood Lake Office
Rte. 1, Box 224
Jamestown, ND 58401
(701) 252-4681
  Primitive camping; permit required for
  horseback riding
          BW, C, H, HR, MB, XC

KNIFE RIVER INDIAN VILLAGES NATIONAL HISTORIC SITE
National Park Service
PO Box 9
Stanton, ND 58571-0009
(701) 745-3309   **BW, CK, F, GS, H, I, MT,**
          PA, RA, T, TG, XC

KULM WETLAND MANAGEMENT DISTRICT
U.S. Fish and Wildlife Service
1 First St. SE, PO Box E
Kulm, ND 58456
(701) 647-2866
  Check with office about seasonal abundance of wildlife   **BW, CK, H**

LAKE METIGOSHE STATE PARK
North Dakota Parks and
Recreation Dept.
#2 LMSP
Bottineau, ND 58318-8044
(701) 263-4651   **BT, BW, C, CK, F, H,**
          I, MB, MT, PA, RA, S, T, TG, XC

L	Lodging	**PA**	Picnic Areas	**RC**	Rock Climbing	**TG**	Tours, Guides
MB	Mountain Biking	**RA**	Ranger-led Activities	**S**	Swimming	**XC**	Cross-country Skiing
MT	Marked Trails			**T**	Toilets		

LITTLE MISSOURI NATIONAL GRASSLAND
U.S. Forest Service
McKenzie Ranger District
HCO 2, Box 8, Watford City, ND 58854-9308
(701) 842-2343 (McKenzie Ranger District)
(701) 225-5151 (Medora Ranger District)
**BT, BW, C, CK, F, H,
HR, MB, MT, PA, XC**

LITTLE MISSOURI STATE PARK
North Dakota Parks and Recreation Dept.
1835 E. Bismarck Expwy.
Bismarck, ND 58504
(701) 764-5256 (May–October)
(701) 794-3731 (year-round)   **BW, C, H,
HR,MT, PA, T, TG**

LOSTWOOD NATIONAL WILDLIFE REFUGE
U.S. Fish and Wildlife Service
RR 2, Box 98, Kenmare, ND 58746
(701) 848-2722
Mountain biking on trails only; best time
to visit May–October; winter travel diffi-
cult; most wildlife gone in winter
BW, H, I, MB, MT, T, XC

MINNEWAUKAN FLATS
Devils Lake Area Chamber of Commerce
Rte. 2E, PO Box B79
Devils Lake, ND 58301
(701) 662-4903   **BW, F**

PEMBINA GORGE
North Dakota Game and Fish Dept.
RR 5, Box 281 B
Devils Lake, ND 58301
(701) 662-3617   **BW, H**

SHEYENNE NATIONAL GRASSLANDS
U.S. Forest Service
PO Box 946, Lisbon, ND 58054
(701) 683-4342   **BW, H, HR, MT**

**SMITH GROVE WILDLIFE
MANAGEMENT AREA**
North Dakota Game and Fish Dept.
100 N. Bismarck Expwy.
Bismarck, ND 58501-5095
(701) 328-6300   **BW, H**

SULLY CREEK STATE PRIMITIVE PARK
Fort Abraham Lincoln State Park
RR 2, Box 139, Mandan, ND 58554
(701) 663-9571   **BW, C, CK,
F, H, HR, MT, PA, T**

SULLYS HILL NATIONAL GAME PRESERVE
U.S. Fish and Wildlife Service
PO Box 908, Devils Lake, ND 58301
(701) 766-4272
Includes regional environmental learn-
ing center; day use only; hours vary,
check with office
BW, H, I, MT, RA, T, TG, XC

TETRAULT WOODS STATE FOREST
North Dakota Forest Service
101 5th St., Walhalla, ND 58282
(701) 228-5422 (forest service)
(701) 662-3617 (Game and Fish)
Snowmobiling **BW, CK, H, HR, MB, MT**

THEODORE ROOSEVELT NATIONAL PARK
National Park Service
PO Box 7, Medora, ND 58645
(701) 623-4466
Entry fee May–October; season passes
available   **BW, C, CK, HR,
I, MT, PA, RA, T, TG, XC**

TURTLE MOUNTAINS
North Dakota Game and Fish Dept.
RR 5, Box 281 B
Devils Lake, ND 58301
(701) 662-3617
BW, C, CK, F, H, MT, S, T, XC

TURTLE MOUNTAIN STATE FOREST
North Dakota Forest Service
First and Brander Sts.
Bottineau, ND 58318
(701) 228-5422; (701) 228-3700
**BT, BW, C, F, H, HR,
MB, MT, PA, S, T, XC**

**UPPER SOURIS NATIONAL
WILDLIFE REFUGE**
U.S. Fish and Wildlife Service
RR 1, Box 163, Foxholm, ND 58718
(701) 468-5467
Includes Lake Darling Dam; self-guided
auto-tour route; sharp-tailed grouse
dancing ground observation blinds
BW, CK, F, GS, H, HR, I, MT, PA, T

WAKOPA WILDLIFE MANAGEMENT AREA
North Dakota Game and Fish Dept.
RR 5, Box 281 B
Devils Lake, ND 58301
(701) 662-361   **BW, C, CK, F, H, HR,
MT, PA, S, T, XC**

BT	Bike Trails	**CK**	Canoeing, Kayaking	**F**	Fishing	**HR**	Horseback Riding
BW	Bird-watching			**GS**	Gift Shop		
C	Camping	**DS**	Downhill Skiing	**H**	Hiking	**I**	Information Center

SOUTH DAKOTA

BADLANDS NATIONAL PARK
National Park Service
PO Box 6, Interior, SD 57750
(605) 433-5361; (605) 455-2878 (June 15–
August 20)   **BW, C, GS, H,
HR, I, L, MT, PA, RA, T**

BEAR BUTTE STATE PARK
South Dakota Div. of
Parks and Recreation
PO Box 688, Sturgis, SD 57785
(605) 347-5240
    Entry fee for east section; horseback rid-
ing and mountain biking limited to Cen-
tennial Trail in west section; tours by
prearrangement   **BT, BW, C, CK, DS, F,
GS, H, HR, I, MB, MT, PA, T, TG, XC**

BLACK ELK WILDERNESS
Black Hills National Forest
RR 2, Box 200, Custer, SD 57730
(605) 673-2251
    Primitive camping; mechanized travel
prohibited   **BW, C, F, H, HR, MT, RC**

BLACK HILLS NATIONAL FOREST
U.S. Forest Service
Rte. 2, Box 200
Custer, SD 57730
(605) 673-2251
    Information center at Pactola Lake,
May–September   **BT, BW, C, CK, F,
H, HR, I, MB, MT, PA, RA, RC, S, T, XC**

BUFFALO GAP NATIONAL GRASSLAND
U.S. Forest Service
PO Box 425
Wall, SD 57790
(605) 279-2125
    Primitive camping; rock hounding
**BT, BW, C, F, GS,
H, HR, I, MB, T, TG**

CRAZY HORSE MEMORIAL
Avenue of the Chiefs
Crazy Horse, SD 57730-9506
(605) 673-4681
    Entry fee   **GS, H, I, T, TG**

CUSTER NATIONAL FOREST
U.S. Forest Service
PO Box 2556, Billings, MT 59103
(406) 657-6361   **BT, BW, C, DS, F, H, HR,
MB, MT, PA, T, XC**

CUSTER STATE PARK
South Dakota Game, Fish and Parks Dept.
HC 83, Box 70
Custer, SD 57730
(605) 255-4515; (605) 255-4464
    Entry fee   **BT, BW, C, F, GS, H, HR, I,
L, MB, MT, PA, RA, RC, S, T, XC**

FARM ISLAND STATE RECREATIONAL AREA
South Dakota Div. of Parks and Recreation
1301 Farm Island Rd.
Pierre, SD 57501
(605) 224-5605   **BT, BW, C, CK, F, H,
MB, MT, PA, S, T, XC**

FRENCH CREEK NATURAL AREA
Custer State Park
HC 83, Box 70, Custer, SD 57730
(605) 255-4515; (605) 255-4464
    Entry fee   **BT, BW, C, F, H, HR, MB, T**

JEWEL CAVE NATIONAL MONUMENT
National Park Service
RR 1, Box 60AA
Custer, SD 57730
(605) 673-2288
    Scenic tour (723 steps); candlelight tour;
spelunking tour (reservations required,
and spelunkers must fit through an 8½ x
24 inch crawl space)   **I, MT, PA, T, TG**

JOSEPH NICOLLET TOWER AND INTERPRETIVE CENTER
Heritage Museum of Roberts County
PO Box 215, Sisseton, SD 57262-0215
(605) 698-7621; (605) 698-7672
**BT, BW, GS, H, I, MB,
MT, PA, T, TG, XC**

KARL E. MUNDT NATIONAL WILDLIFE REFUGE
U.S. Fish and Wildlife Service
c/o Lake Andes National
Wildlife Refuge Complex
RR1, Box 77, Lake Andes, SD 57356
(605) 487-7603
    Closed to public use

LACREEK NATIONAL WILDLIFE REFUGE
U.S. Fish and Wildlife Service
HC 5, Box 114, Martin, SD 57551
(605) 685-6508
    Roads often very muddy and slippery in
rain or closed by winter weather
BW, C, F, H, MT, PA, S, T

L	Lodging	**PA**	Picnic Areas	**RC**	Rock Climbing	**TG**	Tours, Guides
MB	Mountain Biking	**RA**	Ranger-led Activities	**S**	Swimming	**XC**	Cross-country Skiing
MT	Marked Trails			**T**	Toilets		

LA FRAMBOISE ISLAND NATURAL AREA
U.S. Army Corps of Engineers
Oahe Project
28563 Powerhouse Rd.
Pierre, SD 57501
(605) 224-5862   BT, BW, CK, F,
                              H, MB, MT, PA, T, XC

LEMMON PETRIFIED WOOD PARK
City of Lemmon, Park Board
303 1st Ave. W
Lemmon, SD 57638
(605) 374-5114
   Camping and other facilities located
   nearby   BW, GS, H, I, T, TG

LEWIS AND CLARK LAKE VISITOR CENTER
U.S. Army Corps of Engineers
PO Box 710, Yankton, SD 57078
(402) 667-7873, ext. 3249
                        BW, GS, I, MT, RA, TG

LITTLE BEND NATURAL AREA
U.S. Army Corps of Engineers
Oahe Project
28563 Powerhouse Rd.
Pierre, SD 57501
(605) 224-5862   BW, C, CK, F,
                           H, PA, T, XC

MAMMOTH SITE OF HOT SPRINGS
PO Box 692, Hot Springs, SD 57747-0692
(605) 745-6017   I, T, TG

MOUNT RUSHMORE NATIONAL MEMORIAL
National Park Service
PO Box 268, Keystone, SD 57751
(605) 574-2523   BW, GS, H, I,
                           RA, RC, T, TG

MUSEUM OF GEOLOGY
South Dakota School of
Mines and Technology
501 E. St. Joseph St.
Rapid City, SD 57701
(605) 394-2467
   Tours by prearrangement GS, I, PA, T, TG

**NATIONAL GRASSLANDS
VISITOR CENTER**
U.S. Forest Service
PO Box 425
Wall, SD 57790
(605) 279-2125   BT, BW, C, F,
                           GS, H, HR, I, T

NORBECK WILDLIFE PRESERVE
Black Hills National Forest
RR 2, Box 200
Custer, SD 57730
(605) 673-2251
   No off-road vehicle travel
                        BW, C, CK, F, H, HR,
                        MT, PA, RC, S, T, XC

NORTH AND SOUTH CAVE HILLS
Custer National Forest
Sioux Ranger District
PO Box 37, Camp Crook, SD 57724
(605) 797-4432   BW, H, PA

PONCA STATE PARK
Nebraska Game and Parks Commission
PO Box 688, Ponca, NE 68770
(402) 755-2284
   Vehicle entry fee   BW, C, F, GS, H, HR,
                        I, MT, PA, S, T, XC

REYNOLDS PRAIRIE
Black Hills National Forest
Rte. 16 E., Box 23939
Hill City, SD 57745
(605) 574-2534   BT, BW, C, CK, F, H,
                           HR, MB, MT, PA, S, T, XC

SAGE CREEK WILDERNESS AREA
Badlands National Park
PO Box 6, Interior, SD 57750
(605) 433-5361
   Primitive camping; pit toilets
                           BW, C, PA, T

SAMUEL H. ORDWAY PRAIRIE
The Nature Conservancy
HCR 1, Box 16
Leola, SD 57456
(605) 439-3475   BW, H, MT

SAND LAKE NATIONAL WILDLIFE REFUGE
U.S. Fish and Wildlife Service
39650 Sand Lake Drive
Columbia, SD 57433
(605) 885-6320   BW, F, I, PA, T, XC

SICA HOLLOW STATE PARK
South Dakota Div. of Parks
and Recreation
RR 2, Box 94
Lake City, SD 57247
(605) 448-5701   BT, BW, H, HR,
                           MB, MT, PA, T, XC

BT Bike Trails	**CK** Canoeing, Kayaking	**F** Fishing	**HR** Horseback Riding
BW Bird-watching	**DS** Downhill Skiing	**GS** Gift Shop	
C Camping		**H** Hiking	**I** Information Center

SLIM BUTTES
Custer National Forest
Sioux Ranger District
PO Box 37, Camp Crook, SD 57724
(605) 797-4432   **BW, C, F, H, HR, PA**

SPEARFISH CANYON
Black Hills National Forest
2014 N. Main St.
Spearfish, SD 57783
(605) 642-4622   **BW, C, F, H, I,
MT, PA, T, XC**

**SPEARFISH CANYON NATURAL HISTORY
AND CULTURAL CENTER**
HC 27, Box 1387
Spearfish Canyon, SD 57754-9725
(605) 584-2070   **BT, BW, C, DS, F, GS,
H, HR, I, L, MB, MT, PA, RC, T, XC**

WAUBAY NATIONAL WILDLIFE REFUGE
U.S. Fish and Wildlife Service
RR 1, Box 39
Waubay, SD 57273
(605) 947-4521   **BW, I, MT, PA, T**

WIND CAVE NATIONAL PARK
National Park Service
RR 1, Box 190-WCNP
Hot Springs, SD 57747
(605) 745-4600   **BW, C, GS, H, I,
MT, PA, RA, T, TG**

ABOVE: *On a sunny afternoon in 1904, a gentleman and two ladies enjoy
a fishing expedition along the Big Sioux River in eastern South Dakota.*

L	Lodging	**PA**	Picnic Areas	**RC**	Rock Climbing
MB	Mountain Biking	**RA**	Ranger-led Activities	**S**	Swimming
MT	Marked Trails			**T**	Toilets

TG	Tours, Guides	
XC	Cross-country Skiing	**277**

INDEX

Index

PHOTOGRAPHY CREDITS

All photographs by Tom Bean except for the following:
viii, right: Frank Oberle, Saint Charles, MO
ix, left: Scott Nielsen, Superior, WI
xiv: Bell Museum of Natural History, University of Minnesota
5: Rod Planck/Dembinsky Photo Associates (DPA), Owosso, MI
9: Joslyn Art Museum, Omaha, NE, Gift of the Enron Art Foundation (NA 68)
20: National Museum of American Art, Smithsonian Institution, Gift of Mrs. Joseph Harrison, Jr., Washington, D.C. (#1985.66.337)
22: Glenn D. Chambers, Columbia, MO
23, top: Henry Holdsworth/The Wildlife Collection, Brooklyn, NY
23, bottom: Scott Nielsen, Superior, WI
24: John Shaw, Colorado Springs, CO
27: Paul Rezendes, South Royalston, MA
28: Dominique Braud/DPA
32: Carl R. Sams II, Milford, MI
34, bottom: Ken Deitcher/The Wildlife Collection
37, left: Bruce Montagne, Milford, MI
38: A. Blake Gardner, Westminster, VT
40: Minnesota Historical Society, Saint Paul, MN
44: Bruce Montagne, Milford, MI
46: Carl R. Sams II, Milford, MI
47: Robert Lankinen/The Wildlife Collection
48, left: Tom Vezo/The Wildlife Collection
58: Bates Littlehales, Arlington, VA
67: National Museum of American Art, Smithsonian Institution, Gift of Mrs. Joseph Harrison, Jr., Washington, D.C. (# 1985.66.374)
70: Thomas D. Mangelsen/Images of Nature, Jackson, WY
74: John Shaw, Colorado Springs, CO
76: Gary Meszaros/DPA
81: Henry Holdsworth/The Wildlife Collection
88, top: Leonard Lee Rue III, Blairstown, NJ
88, bottom: Len Rue, Jr., Blairstown, NJ
98, left: Michael S. Quinton, Slana, AK
98, right: Bruce Montagne, Milford, MI
103, bottom: Rod Planck/DPA
107: Jim Battles/DPA
112: National Archives of Canada, Ottawa, Canada (#C-40168)
116: Michael S. Quinton, Slana, AK
126: John Shaw, Colorado Springs, CO
138: John Cancalosi, Tucson, AZ
146: Bates Littlehales, Arlington, VA
150, top left: Martin Harvey/The Wildlife Collection
150, top right: Barbara Gerlach, Chatham, MI
150, bottom left: Alan G. Nelson/DPA
150, bottom right: Barbara Gerlach/DPA
154, top: Robert Villani, Merrick, NY
154, bottom: Carl R. Sams II, Milford, MI
162: Barbara Gerlach, Chatham, MI
166: Frank Oberle, Saint Charles, MO
170: Carl R. Sams II/DPA
173: Theodore Roosevelt Collection, Harvard College Library, Cambridge, MA
197: Sharon Cummings/DPA
198, top: John Cancalosi, Tucson, AZ
198, bottom: Gary Meszaros/DPA
204, 205: Buffalo Bill Historical Center, Cody, WY
210, 223: John Hendrickson, Clipper Mills, CA
224: George E. Stewart/DPA
236, top: Frank Oberle, Saint Charles, MO
254-255: Library of Congress, Washington, D.C. (LC-USZ62-99672)
277: South Dakota State Historical Society, Pierre, SD
Back Cover: Scott Nielsen (duck); Tom Bean (blazing star,bison)

ACKNOWLEDGMENTS

The editors gratefully acknowledge the professional assistance of Tish Fila, Susan Kirby, and Patricia Woodruff. We wish to thank those site managers and naturalists whose time and commitment contributed to this volume. The following consultants also helped in the preparation of this volume: John Bluemle, North Dakota Geological Survey; Robert Dana, Plant Ecologist, Minnesota Department of Natural Resources; Hannah Dunevitz, Plant Ecologist, Minnesota Department of Natural Resources; Alexis Duxbury, North Dakota Game and Fish Department; John E. Grassy; David J. Ode, Natural Heritage Program, South Dakota Game, Fish, and Parks Department; Dallas Rhodes, Professor and Chair of Geology, Whittier College; Kurt Rusterholz, Forest Ecologist, Minnesota Department of Natural Resources; Don Schwert, North Dakota State University; John Tester, University of Minnesota Ecology Department.